NEW ENGLAND REMEMBERS

The Cocoanut Grove Fire

Stephanie Schorow

Robert J. Allison, Series Editor

Commonwealth Editions
Beverly, Massachusetts

For Marty Sheridan
and Dotty Myles

ISBN-13: 978-1-889833-88-0
ISBN-10: 1-889833-88-6

Library of Congress Cataloging-in-Publication Data
Schorow, Stephanie.
  The Cocoanut Grove fire / Stephanie Schorow.
    p. cm. — (New England remembers)
  Includes bibliographical references and index.
  ISBN 1-889833-88-6
  1. Cocoanut Grove (Boston, Mass.)—Fire, 1942. 2. Fires—Massachusetts—Boston—History—20th century. 3. Boston (Mass.)—History—20th century. 4. Boston (Mass.)—Buildings, structures, etc. I. Title. II. Series.
  F73.8.C62S34 2005
  974.4'61'042—dc22   2004026444

Cover and interior design by Laura McFadden, laura.mcfadden@rcn.com

Printed in the United States

Commonwealth Editions
266 Cabot Street, Beverly, Massachusetts 01915
www.commonwealtheditions.com

Front cover photo: The Cocoanut Grove on the night of the fire, courtesy of the *Boston Herald*
Back cover photo: Interior of the nightclub, courtesy of Bill Noonan
Author photo by Renee DeKona

New England Remembers series
Robert J. Allison, Series Editor
The Hurricane of 1938
The Big Dig
Sacco and Vanzeti
Lizzie Borden

The "New England Remembers" logo features a photo of the Thomas Pickton House, Beverly, Massachusetts, used courtesy of the Beverly Historical Society.

CONTENTS

The squat tough little building, which is known on Boston's records as No. 13-17 Piedmont St. and to the wide world as the Cocoanut Grove, has passed through successive stages of ambition, drudgery, prosperity and splendor. . . . For fifteen years adults of all ages and fortune purchased illusion within its ornate walls, pausing for a moment of artificial uplift before moving on again—even as you and I. . . . Yet the Cocoanut Grove had another character behind its external glitter, one that its casual patrons who ate $2 dinners and swallowed 50-cent drinks never saw with an outward eye. Behind the screen of colored lights, soft music, pretty girls and moonbeams there [were] the moving shadows of mystery which ran the full gamut of mischief, from swindler to murder to questionable manipulation.

—Austen Lake, Boston Record American,
December 14, 1942

FOREWORD

It was the deadliest fire in New England's history. Shortly after ten o'clock on the night of November 28, 1942, a fire raged through the Cocoanut Grove nightclub in Boston's South End. Within twelve minutes, nearly five hundred people were dead or mortally wounded. Half an hour after receiving the first alarm, the Boston Fire Department had extinguished the fire.

Why was the fire so deadly? What caused it? Who were the victims? Who was responsible? For more than half a century, survivors, many haunted by unbearable memories of that night, have tried to find answers to these and other questions. Journalist Stephanie Schorow examines the Cocoanut Grove fire, telling the story of one of New England's premier nightclubs, and the tragic night that made its name synonymous with horror and devastation. She sorts through the myths and the facts, introducing us to the men and women who died that night, to those who survived, to the doctors who developed new ways of treating burn victims.

In the fire's aftermath, Boston enacted a new building and fire code to prevent another tragedy on this scale. Boston also forbade any nightclub in the city to carry the name "Cocoanut Grove." But the name lives on. New England remembers the Cocoanut Grove fire.

Robert J. Allison, Series Editor
Boston, Massachusetts

INTRODUCTION

The night of November 28, 1942, is seared into the collective memory of Boston. A fast-moving fire roared through the popular Cocoanut Grove nightclub on what was meant to be a festive Saturday evening, leaving more than five hundred people dead, dying, or maimed for life. The inferno reached deep into the city's social structure—its politics, medical care, law enforcement, and religious life—and touched nearly everyone in the Boston area that day, even those who had never set foot in the club. Mention "Cocoanut Grove" to most long-time Massachusetts residents and tales flood out, of great-uncles and aunts who died in or escaped from the fire, of grandmothers who nursed patients, of grandfathers who fought the blaze, or relatives who, amazingly enough, were at the club that night but left early. And yet, for decades, many victims and witnesses could not speak of what they saw or experienced; their silence has helped to create a mystique about the fire, an aura of a holocaust too terrible to imagine.

In sheer numbers, the Cocoanut Grove falls short of the devastating 1903 Iroquois Theatre fire in Chicago, which killed more than six hundred, and the collapse of the World Trade Center towers in a terrorist attack on September 11, 2001. The Grove's impact, however, extends beyond mere statistics. Doctors and nurses, faced with the medical battle of their lives, developed better treatments for burns and lung injuries—treatments still in use today. The fire led to tougher fire safety codes and more stringent enforcement of longstanding regulations. The investigation into the fire's causes and trial of its owner set legal precedents for the culpability of those who do not maintain buildings properly or let expediency stand in the way of safety.

Still, to dwell on the "good" that came of the fire does disservice to its victims and the lives of promise lost in a few moments of terror. Much about the fire remains a mystery, not least of which is how it actually started. Among its professional and amateur historians are Jack Deady of Bedford, New Hampshire, whose father, Philip Deady, investigated the fire for the state fire marshal's office, and retired firefighter

Charles Kenney, whose firefighter father fought the blaze. These two men make it a point to warn fledgling fire researchers that the Cocoanut Grove is a story that never ends, that the fire has a terrible power to pull the curious into a labyrinth of outrage and subterfuge. Because many of those responsible for the Grove disaster took their secrets to the grave, there has been little chance to write a final chapter to this never-ending tale or to find closure to the tragedy.

The fire's bitterest legacy is, perhaps, that its lessons must be endlessly repeated. On February 20, 2003, a rock band's indoor fireworks ignited the Station, a Rhode Island nightclub. In the ensuing panic, a hundred people were killed or died later from their injuries. The tragedy's resemblance to the Cocoanut Grove was uncanny; in each, flames spread with horrifying speed through the extraordinarily flammable interiors, and patrons packed into the buildings jammed available exits.

The greatest temptation in assessing tragedy is to infuse it with meaning, to promote the belief that something so bad must be a step to a greater good. The heroics of the Cocoanut Grove nightclub fire—and there were, indeed, some heroes—have assumed mythical status, and the odd coincidences of luck are snatched up as evidence of divine intervention. But the ongoing fascination with the Cocoanut Grove does not stem from the heroics of a few but from the many strange threads of chance and circumstance that were woven together to produce one of Boston's worst disasters.

PROLOGUE

Outside, it's bitter cold. Inside the nightclub, the joint is jumping. Anxious for a chance to take a break from the gloom of winter and the worries of war, crowds of people—young and old—hurry along Piedmont Street, in the city's theater district, heading for the revolving door under the Cocoanut Grove sign that reaches toward the sky. They anticipate the loud buzz of conversations, the cocktail-fueled laughter, the air saturated with cigarette smoke and perfume. They will check their coats and stroll into the main dining room, a faux South Seas paradise in chilly Boston, with fake palm trees, rattan furniture, and chairs upholstered with a striking zebra pattern. Maybe they'll be lucky—they might get seats in the area reserved for celebrities, a raised terrace set back from the main stage. Who knows who could be there? Cowboy star Buck Jones was in town, wasn't he? There was a new singer, too. Dotty Myles—only a teenager, but said to already be a star. Sure, it was expensive—an order of a half dozen oysters was 40 cents, broiled scrod was 80 cents, a baked lobster was $2.25, a tenderloin steak was $2. But it was the Cocoanut Grove, after all.

A night on the town. That was the plan for many Bostonians on November 28, 1942. That is, until they walked through the revolving door and found the club too crowded for comfort and the heat too high for enjoyment. The coatroom was so full that coats were stacked on the floor. The dance floor was shrinking as waiters tried to squeeze even more tables into the main dining area. Disappointed, would-be merry makers left—to seek another club or restaurant or maybe call it a night. They would not realize until the next day how lucky they had been.

CHAPTER ONE

Boston's Number One Glitter Spot

I n 1942 entertainer Mickey Alpert was Mr. Cocoanut Grove, not only because he once owned the place but because his ebullient personality and natural wit as master of ceremonies made his name synonymous with the nightspot. More charming than conventionally handsome, and blessed with an ambition for center stage, Alpert had been the driving force behind the birth of the Cocoanut Grove. His dreams of bright lights and applause helped turn a former garage into Boston's number one glitter spot.

Born Milton Irving Alpert in 1904, Mickey grew up in Roxbury, where he worked in the furniture business. He started singing—mainly on radio ads for the furniture store—and acted in local theater productions. "I sold furniture in the daytime and broadcast at night. You might call it double in brass," he later told a reporter. The ambitious Alpert found a kindred soul in bandleader Jacques Renard (born Jacob Stavisky), an excellent musician and bandleader who had already developed a following in the Boston area. The pair wanted their own nightclub, a vision that led them to an unassuming concrete block building at 17 Piedmont Street, just outside Boston's theater district on the edge of Bay Village, one of the city's oldest neighborhoods. The place had been built as a garage and was later converted into a film distribution company. In the late 1920s, with legal assistance from Mickey's brother,

The Cocoanut Grove, on Piedmont Street near the Theater District. The humble exterior seems to belie the club's reputation as Boston's number one glitter spot. (Courtesy of the **Boston Herald***)*

The interior of the club was designed to evoke a tropical paradise, with palm trees and a ceiling painted to resemble a starry sky. Angelo Lippi was the maitre d'. (Courtesy of the National Fire Protection Association)

George, then youngest-ever first assistant district attorney for Suffolk County, they began planning to turn the one-story structure into a premier nightspot.

The pair got a boost when, vacationing in Maine, they met a generous but somewhat mysterious California businessman named Jack Berman, who, hearing the young men talk about creating Boston's hottest night spot, put up the money for the venture. Berman shared their enthusiasm for building a top-notch club, and money flowed from his wallet as if he owned his own greenback printing press. Reuben Bodenhorn, then a famed nightclub decorator, was hired to design the interior and give the club its "look"; Bodenhorn envisioned a tropical paradise to enliven cold New Englanders. He covered the walls with imitation leather or leatherette and dotted a large main dining and dancing room with fake palm trees. The ceiling was painted to suggest a night sky and, for an even more exotic touch, the entire roof could be rolled back on a hot summer night for dancing under the real night sky. The main dining room featured a rolling stage for the band and a raised terrace that simulated a Spanish courtyard and was reserved for important guests and celebrities. Hired as maitre d' was Angelo Lippi, known as "The Count," or "Signor," whose waxed moustache and ever-unruffled demeanor in the face of celebrities or unruly drunks would become legendary. Berman reportedly spent eighty-five thousand dollars on the remodeling; he even suggested the name "Cocoanut Grove," after the similarly named club in his home base of California. George Alpert, however, insisted that the club strictly adhere to liquor laws; setups were fine, actual booze was not. Prohibition was the law, ratified by the Eighteenth Amendment in 1919. But Alpert and Renard were confident great entertainment alone would draw the crowds.

Curiously, Berman wanted to remain in the background, leaving Alpert and Renard to take front stage, as both the managers and the main attraction. The pair thought that was odd, but as long as the cash flowed, they didn't question Berman's largesse. Three days before the club was to open, however, the benefactor bubble burst. To their horror, Alpert and Renard learned that Berman was actually Jack Bennett, a partner in the Julian Petroleum Company, under arrest by the feds for manipulating the oil stock market and fleecing millions from investors. The Grove's munificent benefactor turned out to be a con man, eager

3

to launder his ill-gotten gains. Panicked and not even sure who owned the club now, Alpert and Renard called in brother George, who used his legal finesse to work out a deal to keep the club open. In a blitz of extravagance on October 27, 1927, the club welcomed its first customers. "The whole town turned out," as Lippi recalled years later in a newspaper interview. "It was Prohibition, of course, and we served only soft drinks," he added primly. "Setups at corkage prices were provided, however."

Despite the shaky start, the club appeared to be a success. Renard, the better musician, brought in the music lovers. Alpert added the pizzazz, winning acclaim for his stage style; local critics called him "a second Al Jolson." Cocktails, however, proved to be a more essential ingredient than glamour. Under the grip of Prohibition and particularly after the stock market crash of 1929—when the country really needed a drink—the club began to struggle. Within two years, the dream had dissolved into bitter acrimony between Renard and Alpert and the club teetered on the brink of bankruptcy. Moreover, Alpert decided he wanted out; Boston was too confining—he wanted to seek fame in the even-brighter lights of New York City. George Alpert wanted to sell the club and be done with it.

Enter Charles "King" Solomon. A heavyset, round-faced thug, Solomon ran liquor and dope smuggling and other businesses spoken about only in whispers. With his connections to the Murder Incorporated wise guys in New York City, he was untouchable in Boston, "short of a particularly messy murder," as *Record American* reporter Austen Lake later put it. Through his lawyer, Barnett Welansky, Solomon made an offer to the Alperts that they decided they could not refuse. For ten thousand dollars, the club passed into Solomon's hands in 1931. Renard tried to put up a legal fight, but his stock in the club was judged worthless and the sulking musician decamped to a rival nightclub.

The Russian-born King wanted the Cocoanut Grove for his personal showcase. According to Lake, Solomon was "at the peak of his crime renaissance, with a complete sideline of alki-cooking, morphine, heroin, cocaine and the dandruff-like little granules which produce delirious uproar. He hogged the bail-bond market, owned a large loan shark company at usurious rate, held full partnership in the white slave

Souvenirs from the Cocoanut Grove—ironically, matches. (Courtesy of Kathy Alpert and Jack Deady)

industry, a cut in a growing lottery racket and drivers and such like et ceteras built on human mischief." Solomon also owned (secretly or not) other hotels and clubs in Boston and New York City. But Solomon made the Grove his prize pet and, as an added benefit, was supplied with a means to launder more ill-gotten revenues.

The best of vaudeville came to the Cocoanut Grove stage: Texas Guinan and her "Hello, Suckers" comedy review; Sophie Tucker; Gilda Gray, the original "HulaGirl"; and others. Pretty girls were always seated at Solomon's table. Other stars that lit up the club were Jimmy Durante, Rudy Vallee, and Guy Lombardo. "Sally Rand, ran 'round without her rompers," as Lake quipped. Solomon retained Angelo Lippi as the maitre d', even though (as Lippi later said) Solomon could be slow with a paycheck (one didn't bother the King with something as trivial as one's daily wages). There were other dodges. Lippi was for a time listed as the president and treasurer of the club's corporation, although he later said he never attended a board meeting.

Despite the genial face he displayed to patrons, Solomon was a ruthless, streetwise gangster. His darkest legacy—a tradition that doomed patrons decades later—arose from his deepest fears: he made sure exit doors to the club were locked inside and out. No one could sneak in on him and no one—neither patron nor employee—could run out on a bill. Solomon's paranoia was justified. In January 1933, he was holding court at the Cotton Club in Roxbury, possibly another one of his holdings, when, according to newspaper reports, a group of men hustled him into the bathroom and shots rang out. The assailants fled and Solomon staggered out clutching his stomach. "The dirty rats got me," he croaked before collapsing—at least, that's how the Boston press put it.

As befits a fallen gangster, King was nearly "bankrupt"; the final audit of his kingdom put its worth at only $458.22. The Cocoanut Grove was listed among his assets as having "no value." Quickly—with a speed that intrigued later investigators of the fire—the ownership of the club passed from Solomon's widow, Bertha, to Barnett Welansky, "the bland monosyllabic young lawyer," as Lake dubbed him, who represented Solomon.

Welansky was, as reporters later wrote, "a typical American success story." Born in Boston in 1896, as one of six children, Welansky grew up an ambitious, energetic kid with a yearning to be a lawyer. He sold papers to earn money for college and eventually got his law degree in 1918 from Boston University and his master's degree a year later. After being admitted to the bar in 1919, he joined the prestigious practice of Herbert F. Callahan. Welansky's younger brother, James, took a different route in life. James was a player in the city's nightclub scene; he was managing Boston's Metropolitan Hotel when a notorious racketeer and gambler, David "Beano" Breen, was shot to death in the hotel lobby in December 1937. James promptly skipped town, only to resurface in Florida two months later, claiming that he had merely decided to take a long-planned vacation . . . without luggage and under an assumed name. Arrested for the murder by prosecutors who claimed that he and Breen had run a gambling operation, James Welansky insisted that he did nothing and saw nothing and a grand jury refused to indict him.

Barnett Welansky seemed to represent a more respectable side of the family. He ran the Grove like a business, not a showcase. He bought adjoining property and expanded the club; booking stars was secondary to making profits. Rose Gnecco Ponzi was hired to keep the books. (Rose's ex-husband, Charles Ponzi, had the dubious distinction of creating the financial scam that bears his name: the Ponzi scheme.) Yet the records were vague—deliberately so—on just who owned the club: the Grove's property was registered as owned by Jennie Welansky, Welansky's sister, and his brother Benjamin replaced Lippi as president in 1933; Barnett was listed as president-treasurer only after Benjamin went into the army in 1942. The Welansky era got a boost from Congress when Prohibition was repealed in December 1933. The night the first legal drink was served became legendary. According to the requirements of the law, the Grove could not begin to build a bar until noontime of the day the law was repealed. So work began at noon and by nine o'clock the bar was ready—perhaps the fastest-built bar in the city of Boston. Even as carpenters hammered in the finishing touches, patrons were toasting the death of Prohibition. Pressed to make his first-ever speech, the suave Lippi put it simply: "The bar is open."

Shrewd businessman that he was, Welansky didn't want the Grove's glitter to fade entirely. He brought back Mickey Alpert as master of ceremonies. Alpert had played clubs in New York and acted in a few Broadway shows. He had also met a blonde dancer, Katherine Rand, now his steady girl. But nothing equaled his early success at the Grove, and the Boston boy came home where his smile and winning personality won back fans. Alpert now worked with bandleader Bernardo "Bernie" Fazioli, who had a lineup of top-notch musicians. Other regular entertainers included singer Billy Payne—a good friend of

*Emcee Mickey Alpert, singer Billy Payne, maitre d' Angelo Lippi, and an unidentified man. (Courtesy of the **Boston Herald**)*

Alpert's—rowdy pianist/singer Goody Goodelle, and ethereal songstress Grace McDermott.

Welansky turned the club into a complex. In 1938, he built the downstairs Melody Lounge, a dimly lit piano bar that retained a speakeasy atmosphere. It was appointed with a circular bar, a piano stand, and fake palm trees. Folds of fabric were suspended about eighteen inches below a concrete ceiling, to further enhance the sense of intimacy. It provided another alternative to the main dining room. Off the main dining room Welansky installed the Caricature Bar, Boston's longest bar—forty-eight feet—in a room festooned with drawings of celebrities. As business boomed, Welansky bought an adjoining three-story building, and in early November 1942 he opened a new cocktail lounge on the first floor, popularly called the Broadway Lounge. The addition brought the total square footage of the club's ground level to more than 9,700 feet. Indeed, the bland lawyer Welansky succeeded in turning the club into "Boston's number one glitter spot and the axis around which Boston's night life revolved," Lake wrote. Welansky supervised almost every aspect of the club, arranging for all licenses and alterations and even looking for floor-show acts when he was in New York on business.

Like Solomon, Welansky insisted on limited access in—and out—of the club. While, years later, many of his employees recalled him as personable and fair, "Trust no one" seemed to be his operating motto. Bookkeeper Katherine Swett feared his wrath—that fear would lead to her death. Welansky's nephew, Daniel Weiss, hired as a bartender in the Melody Lounge, knew nothing would upset his uncle more than losing track of his receipts. Indeed, Welansky seemed determined not to let a single employee skip out on a bill. Customers had only one entrance into the main part of the club, under an archway on Piedmont Street and through a revolving door. Another exit to Piedmont Street led from a cloakroom, but it was blocked by shelves. An emergency exit was located down a small hallway at the top of the stairs that led to the Melody Lounge. The door was equipped with a "panic" or "crash" bar designed to open the door from pressure inside the building. In the main dining room on the Shawmut Street side, a double door was hidden by curtains, and a row of windows was covered with wood panels. There were service entrances in the basement and behind the orchestra stage, but they were locked inside and out at night. The only public entrance and exit to the Broadway Lounge was through one door on Broadway that led into a small vestibule and then through another door.

On November 20, the Cocoanut Grove was inspected by Boston fire prevention lieutenant Frank Linney, who declared the club's condition "good." Linney determined the club had an adequate number of exits and the interior decorations were not flammable. He even held a match to one of the palm trees; it did not ignite. Eight days later, Linney's assessment would be proved horribly wrong.

CHAPTER TWO

The Day of the Fire

Despite the war and the early winter chill, Boston greeted the dawn of November 28, 1942, with eager anticipation. Today at Fenway Park, Boston College's undefeated football team would play Holy Cross of Worcester. Naturally, Boston College fans expected their team to win, and BC officials were already planning for their trip to the Sugar Bowl. Bowl. Tonight—after the expected victory—they would hoist their glasses to the team at the Cocoanut Grove nightclub, the best spot in town. All the players and the coach would be there, along with a host of Boston politicians and leaders. This would be a night to see and be seen basking in Boston's football glory.

The city teemed with sailors and servicemen ready for a last fling before they were sent overseas, and they sought entertainment in the burlesque houses of Boston's notorious Scollay Square, or clubs like the Cocoanut Grove or the Mayfair or the Latin Quarter, where Jacques Renard still reigned. Other Bostonians spent Saturday night at the movies or the theater.

Bernie Fazioli, the Cocoanut Grove music director, had put together a band of experienced and up-and-coming musicians, including Al Willet and Romeo Ferrara on sax, Al Maglitta on drums, and Jack Lesberg on bass. Just twenty-two years old, Lesberg, a Boston native and the son of Russian immigrants, was following in the footsteps of his elder brother, David, already a well-known classical musician. Lesberg, however, played the string bass and had developed a talent for jazz. He had cut short a tour with the Muggsy Spanier band to be with his ailing parents in Boston, but counted himself lucky to have found a gig at the Cocoanut Grove, the city's swank hot spot.

Boston was then a great training ground for many performers. Among them was Dotty Myles, a seventeen-year-old singer with a lilting voice and a natural, fresh-faced beauty who hoped the Cocoanut Grove would be her stepping-stone to stardom. Born Dorothy Metzger in New York City on West 101st Street, she was taking voice lessons by the time she was nine years old, and by twelve she was winning voice contests. In her late teens, she started singing in nightclubs and finally got the call she was hoping for—to audition for Jimmy Dorsey himself. To prepare, she booked her first full-time professional appearance, a four-week stint at the Cocoanut Grove, beginning in early November. The reaction—from audiences and other musicians—was everything a girl could want. Jack Lesberg, for one, thought she had a terrific voice and was a "straight ahead" hardworking gal. He also thought she was very pretty. Between shows, Dotty caught up on her schoolwork.

But for many, the day didn't go as planned. That afternoon, at Fenway Park, the BC crowd watched their football dreams evaporate as Holy Cross beat Boston College 55-12. No Sugar Bowl this year. Boston College fans were devastated—the loss, they had to believe, must be a sign of divine displeasure with the Jesuit-run college. With deep regret Boston College officials cancelled their plans for a Cocoanut Grove victory party.

Even if Boston College was down and out, plenty of folks turned out to drink and dance. What was a debacle for Boston was a cause for celebration for twenty-one-year-old John Quinn of Worcester, who had been rooting for Holy Cross: he had just two more days until he had to report back for duty at the U.S. Naval Training Center in Newport, Rhode Island, and he had come to Boston with buddy Dick Vient for some R&R before reporting for duty. Thrilled by the Holy Cross victory, the young men arranged to bring their girls to the Cocoanut Grove that night to celebrate. Vient brought his fiancée Marion Luby; Quinn's steady girl was Gerry Whitehead, whom he had

Publicist Martin Sheridan (right) interviewing cowboy star Buck Jones just hours before the Cocoanut Grove fire. (Courtesy of Martin Sheridan)

loved since his junior year in high school. He knew they would get married after he returned from the war. Tonight they would be together at the Cocoanut Grove.

Married just a few hours earlier, John and Claudia O'Neill were celebrating at the Cocoanut Grove with members of their wedding party. They had planned to leave after the first show, but Lynn Andrews, the club's roving photographer, had snapped their picture and they decided to stick around until it was developed and delivered. Joseph Dreyfus, a medical student and hardly a regular nightclub goer, was there with his wife, Adele, and another couple to have a send-off party for an acquaintance who was going overseas.

Also inside was cowboy star Buck Jones, the star of *Ghost Town Law, Below the Border, Forbidden Trails*, and *Gunman from Bodie*. A real cowboy—born Charles Frederick Gebhard in Indiana in 1894—he had grown up riding horses and worked as a cowhand in Montana. He served with the U.S. Cavalry in the Philippines and worked as an expert rider for various Wild West shows. The work led to stunt jobs in Hollywood westerns, then being churned out conveyor-belt fashion. By the early 1920s the six-foot-tall Jones, with his rugged build and laconic charm, had become a leading man and one of the country's favorite cowboys. His fan club, the Buck Jones Rangers, numbered in the millions and his fan mail piled as high as the Rockies. After appearing in nearly 120 westerns—both silent and talkies—Jones was among the top tier of cowboy stars, in the ranks of Tom Mix, Bronco Bill Anderson, and William S. Hart. In recent years, however, he had been eclipsed by singing cowboys like Gene Autry (a trend he decried to the *New York Times*, saying, "They use 'em to save money on horses and riders and ammunition"). But Jones's manager, Scott Dunlap, had teamed him up with Monogram Pictures, which specialized in low-budget films, and he had just completed *Dawn on the Great Divide* and *West of the Law*, two pictures Monogram and Jones hoped would fend off the singing-cowboy invasion. War bonds sales in Boston coincided with the release of these two "Rough Rider" pictures, and Dunlap hoped the double promotion—war bonds and cowboy pictures—would renew interest in this "old-time cowboy, the sort the kids used to want to grow up to be like," as Jones's publicity described him.

Jones had been tired when their train arrived in Boston the night of November 27, but the fifty-three-year-old cowboy, fighting a cold and eager to get home to California, was tough. He signed autographs for servicemen at the station and met his Boston publicist, a quick-witted young man with thick black-rimmed glasses, Martin Sheridan.

Ink ran in Martin Sheridan's veins. A freelance reporter, he had a knack for writing personality features, particularly about the day's celebrities, from John Dos Passos and George Gershwin to Lilly Dache and Prince Bertil of Sweden. Intimidated? Not this twenty-eight-year-old. "The bigger the person is, I find, the easier he is to handle," he liked to brag. A native Rhode Islander, he knew all the players in Boston, and virtually every other reporter knew Marty. Despite success with his first book on the history of comics, money wasn't exactly flowing in and Marty had a wife to support. So he did freelance publicity work on the side; he'd escort famous people—such as the popular young comedian Bob Hope—around Boston, interview them on radio broadcasts, and snap their pictures. Since he enjoyed meeting people, he didn't mind the work. At the request of Monogram Pictures, he would escort Buck Jones around Boston.

He had Buck's schedule completely mapped out: the next morning they would visit ailing kids at Children's Hospital at 9:30 A.M.; attend a Junior Commando rally at Boston Garden at 11:00 A.M.; and have cocktails and luncheon with theater people and the press at 12:15 P.M. at the Statler Hotel. Sheridan even arranged for the loan of a horse from a Boston police officer and he managed to locate a Samson Spot twenty-foot lariat for Jones. Jones would also watch the BC-Holy Cross football game from mayor Maurice Tobin's box, do a radio interview, and, finally, appear at the Buddies Club.

Sheridan's careful planning for Buck Jones paid off. The Children's Hospital visit was particularly successful; Buck Jones, wearing a large sombrero and cowboy boots, was rapturously greeted by the kids. The radio interview had gone well. Then the schedule took an unexpected turn. In the early evening, Jones taxied to the tony suburb of Newton for a cocktail party with local movie executives. He was now seriously suffering from his cold and asked Sheridan if he could skip his appearance at the Buddies Club. He wanted to go back to his hotel and rest. Sheridan obligingly cancelled the appearance. But the movie bigwigs weren't about to let the cowboy ride off into the sunset without having a bit of his star power rub off on them. They had planned a party at the Cocoanut Grove, and they insisted that Jones come along to the club. Ever the stalwart cowboy, Jones felt he couldn't let them down. Sheridan, on the other hand, was grumpy. He had never been to the Cocoanut Grove and had no desire to go there. Still, he picked up his wife, Connie, who was happy about showing off her new mink coat, and joined the group, which included Edward Ansin, president of Interstate Theatres; Philip Seletsky, of the M&P chain that owned 110 New England theaters; Charles Stern, a New York representative of United Artists Corporation; and Harry Asher, president of Producer Releasing Corporation. Most of them brought their wives. The party, now numbering about thirty, arrived sometime before ten o'clock at the Cocoanut Grove, which was already packed.

They joined couples on their first date, couples celebrating anniversaries, servicemen, and groups of friends out for a night of fun. Among city officials enjoying the club's hospitality—which often included free booze for local politicos—was John Walsh, Boston's civil defense director, who was with a party in the main dining area. Two key players were *not* there that night. Owner Barnett Welansky fell suddenly ill on November 16 and remained hospitalized to recover from a heart condition. The usually unflappable Angelo Lippi was home suffering from arthritis. The lives of all of them were about to be changed irrevocably.

CHAPTER THREE

Into the Inferno

Marty Sheridan was not impressed with his first glimpse of the Cocoanut Grove. The place was too smoky, too noisy, and far too jam-packed—the crowd was later estimated to be at least a thousand, about double the legal capacity. The dance floor was steadily dwindling as waiters tried to fit more and more people in the dining room. Tables were even being set up in the passageway that connected the main dining room with the new lounge. Sheridan's large party had to be shoe-horned into two tables on the raised terrace, the section reserved for celebrities. The waiters couldn't even reach the tables so patrons had to pass dishes and drinks to other tables. Dutifully, although he felt he had already done his job for the day, Sheridan told the Cocoanut Grove staff to tell Mickey Alpert that he should introduce cowboy star Buck Jones. Pressed against a wall, which seemed curiously warm, Sheridan ordered an oyster cocktail and hoped the night would pass quickly.

Above the babble of the crowd, he heard a commotion. "Fight. Fight!!" Probably some football fans had decided to replay the game with their fists, he figured. Then he saw smoke and heard the cry again: "FIRE!" followed by the crackle of unseen flames. "Let's get out of here," he said to his wife, keeping his voice casual. "How about my mink coat?" Connie cried. "To hell with it. Let's take our time and get out of here."

As they—and others—rose in confusion, the club lights went out and Sheridan found himself engulfed by smoke amid shrieks and the crashing sounds of breaking dishes and glasses. As if clubbed by an invisible bat, he passed out. Around him, other people were falling, struck down by a ferocious heat that roared through the club like a fiery tidal wave.

Less than ten minutes earlier, a man in the downstairs Melody Lounge had decided he needed a little more privacy. His name has never been identified, and what happened next has been debated for decades. This much is clear. Shortly after ten o'clock, a man cuddling with a woman in the northwest corner of the packed Melody Lounge reached into a fake palm tree and unscrewed a tiny lightbulb; even the dimly lit Melody Lounge was too bright for him. When bartender John Bradley realized the light was dimmed, he asked a busboy, young Stanley Tomaszewski, to put the light back on. At sixteen years old, Tomaszewski was too young to work legally in the club, but his mother was ailing and he needed the money—$2.47 a night plus tips. So a buddy who worked at the Grove had got him the job. Even as the customer told him jokingly to leave the bulb unscrewed, Stanley dutifully climbed on a chair or a table and reached into the fake palm fronds for the bulb; it came away in his hand. Now, he couldn't see the socket. So he took out a matchbook, lit a match, and located the socket, holding the match in his right hand. When the bulb was secure, he put out the match (possibly by grinding it with his heel) and turned away to go back to work.

About that time patrons in the bar saw a tiny flare or spark in the palm tree. Other witnesses reported seeing a flash. Twenty-six-year-old Maurice Levy of Roxbury saw the top of the palm tree smolder, then puff up and ignite, torching the drapes of material covering the ceiling. Both Bradley and Tomaszewski rushed to the corner and tried to extinguish the fire. Tomaszewski beat it with his hands, to no avail. Some customers thought it was funny, others were simply stunned, and a few started to leave the lounge. Levy grabbed his wife and headed for the stairs. Sensing the confusion, Bradley and Tomaszewski started yelling for people to follow them into the kitchen—they knew there were exits there—as the lounge rapidly filled with smoke and flames.

Behind the bar was Welansky's nephew, twenty-four-year-old Daniel Weiss, a medical student at Boston University. He heard a noise and turned around to what seemed to be an unusual light in the corner.

Realizing that the ceiling was on fire, he pitched a mixing glass of water at the flames, but to no effect. As people started to flee, he felt he couldn't leave his post at the cash register. Coughing and gagging from the smoke, he managed somehow to soak a bar towel with water and held it to his face as he dropped to the floor, where the air seemed better. The smoke had a strange sweet taste that made his nose and throat dry. The sounds of screaming grew louder and louder before fading away.

Instead of following Bradley, most of the crowd ran up the stairs out of the lounge. Some ran to the exit door that led to Piedmont Street, the door with a panic bar. Dozens piled against it, beating on it with all their strength; it refused to budge. (It was later found to be locked and bolted shut.) Others ran for the main exit, the revolving door off the main dining room. Some foolishly stopped to try to retrieve coats. As a crush of increasingly terrified patrons pressed into the revolving door, it spun, ejecting some onto the sidewalk. Then, as the crowd pressed on both sides, the door jammed. Levy, who had lost his wife in the crowd, managed to get out, the last person to do so. When he turned around, the person behind him was being burned alive behind the glass.

When Quinn, Vient, and their girls arrived at the club some time after nine o'clock, they had managed to get a table in the crowded main dining room. A little before ten, on the way to the men's room, Quinn and Vient had noticed the stairway to the Melody Lounge and walked down for a look-see. With the singer on a revolving piano stand, warbling "Never Let a Sailor Get an Inch Above Your Knee," the lounge seemed a better spot than the jammed dining area. They grabbed their girls and had barely made it down the stairs into the Melody Lounge when one side of the room lit up; Quinn could see that one of the fake palm trees was on fire. Quickly, they turned around and started up the stairs, passing what appeared to be a waiter with a fire extinguisher. So it would be over soon, Quinn thought. Almost instantly the waiter rushed back past them. The foursome reached the foyer leading to the main dining room amid an increasingly panicked crowd. Quinn felt a blast of heat sear the back of his neck. Turning, he saw a sheet of bright orange flames that stretched ceiling to floor. He didn't look back again. Ahead of him and Gerry, Dick and Marion seemed to be headed for the coat check. Quinn knew that the main entrance was just to his right but already he sensed people were backing up behind the revolving door. And then the lights went out. The narrow (four-feet-wide) staircase from the Melody Lounge had acted as a chimney, increasing the temperature of the air and sending heat and carbon monoxide upward. The fire moved so fast that the Melody Lounge was engulfed before people in the main dining room were even aware of any trouble.

Around ten, Mickey Alpert was getting ready for the night's second show and the live radio broadcast. He was chatting with singer Billy Payne, who would kick off the evening by singing the national anthem, when someone asked Alpert if he could announce that Buck Jones was in the audience. As he got up, he heard a commotion; "Hey Mickey, it's a fight," Payne said. Turning, he could see fire from the lobby, and then fire seemed to be everywhere. Screams and yells reverberated. A ball of flame, described variously as bright orange or bluish with a yellow cast or bright white, roared through the dining room, rippling along the ceiling, and filled the air with fire before anything had begun to burn, probably drawn by a ventilating fan in the Caricature Bar. Those not felled immediately by the superheated air began to gag on the smoke—thick, acrid, and laced with a strange, sweet smell that stuck in the nose and throat. From the stage, Billy Payne saw a terrific ball of yellow or white flame billowing past the checkroom, past the two telephone booths in the lobby, heading right for him. Payne attempted to calm the crowd but he was pushed aside. Fleeing down the stairs behind the stage toward the kitchen, he covered his mouth with a towel, as he heard someone yelling about getting keys for an outside door. As the smoke surrounded him, Payne started saying his Hail Marys, fearing the end was near. Then he heard an upstairs door being smashed in; he called for people to follow him as he went upstairs where a fireman was pulling people out. "It was all in what seemed like a year but was probably ten minutes," he later told police.

When the cry of fire rang out in the main dining room, Dreyfus, the medical student, stood up, because, as he later said, he had been taught not to panic. He saw a sheet of flames coming across the room. Instinctively, he covered his eyes and almost immediately passed out. He fell to the floor and wasn't discovered for hours. He later woke up in Boston City Hospital, his lungs and trachea damaged and his hands burned to the bone. The rest of his party, including his wife, Adele, were dead. By falling to the floor so quickly, he had breathed cleaner, cooler air while his party got the full brunt of the heat and the fumes.

With their hair on fire and their skin blistering, people scrambled for the only exit they knew—the revolving door, which was jammed, with bodies rapidly piling up behind it. Few knew that across the main dining room, behind draperies on the Shawmut Street side, was a double door. Moreover, the wall itself had three plate-glass windows, but they were covered with a wood veneer. As the fire spread, a fast-thinking waiter wrenched aside the draperies and tried to open the door; it was locked. People converged to try to open it, among them John Walsh, Boston's civil defense director. They managed to open one of the double doors and people began pouring out.

Quinn had made a quick choice. Deciding that the revolving door would quickly jam, he headed for the Shawmut Street door. He pushed Gerry into the middle of the crowd, hoping that they would be squeezed like a tube of toothpaste to the other side. Grabbing Gerry by the waist, he whispered, "Do exactly as I tell you and don't say anything until we get out." Gerry broke that promise only once. They forged ahead into the mob as black smoke filled the room. They would take a step, then Gerry would trip over something, maybe a body, but Quinn did not dare to look down. He concentrated on lifting her to her feet and keeping her steady through the frantic mob of patrons. He saw two tuxedoed men who seemed to be trying to swim out by pulling the hair of people in front of them. Quinn felt his knees buckling. Falling to one knee he put a hand on Gerry's back, determined to push her out with his last strength. It was then she broke the code of silence. "Air," she gasped. Galvanized by that one word, Quinn pushed himself to his feet and, squeezed on both sides, he and Gerry were pushed out the door, landing on the hood of a car without ever touching the sidewalk. The tube-of-toothpaste strategy had worked.

Unfortunately, fire also seeks air. As oxygen in the dining room was depleted, the flames roared toward the Shawmut Street door, turning the precious opening into a roaring blaze, trapping those inside who had not yet escaped. Among them was the young singer Dotty Myles.

She had arrived about nine fifteen, and thought she'd catch a few moments to study her algebra book before she went on stage. About ten o'clock, she saw a strange glow coming from the Melody Lounge

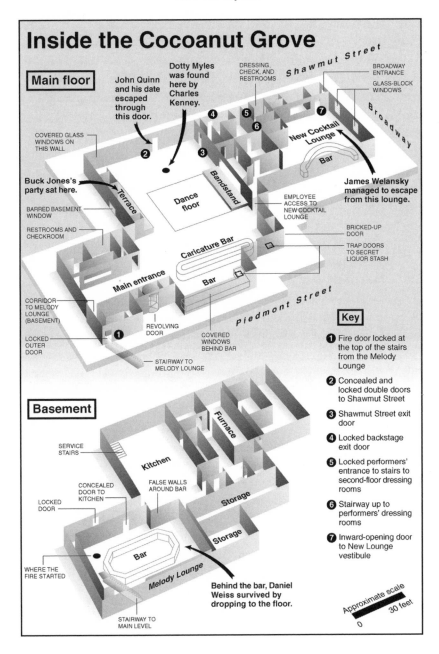

Inside the Cocoanut Grove

Main floor

John Quinn and his date escaped through this door.

Dotty Myles was found here by Charles Kenney.

DRESSING, CHECK, AND RESTROOMS

Shawmut Street

BROADWAY ENTRANCE

GLASS-BLOCK WINDOWS

Broadway

COVERED GLASS WINDOWS ON THIS WALL

New Cocktail Lounge

Bar

4

5

6

7

2

3

Buck Jones's party sat here.

Terrace

Bandstand

Dance floor

EMPLOYEE ACCESS TO NEW COCKTAIL LOUNGE

James Welansky managed to escape from this lounge.

BARRED BASEMENT WINDOW

RESTROOMS AND CHECKROOM

Caricature Bar

BRICKED-UP DOOR

TRAP DOORS TO SECRET LIQUOR STASH

Main entrance

Bar

Piedmont Street

CORRIDOR TO MELODY LOUNGE (BASEMENT)

LOCKED OUTER DOOR

1

REVOLVING DOOR

COVERED WINDOWS BEHIND BAR

STAIRWAY TO MELODY LOUNGE

Basement

Furnace

SERVICE STAIRS

Kitchen

CONCEALED DOOR TO KITCHEN

FALSE WALLS AROUND BAR

Storage

LOCKED DOOR

Storage

Bar

Melody Lounge

WHERE THE FIRE STARTED

Behind the bar, Daniel Weiss survived by dropping to the floor.

STAIRWAY TO MAIN LEVEL

Key

1 Fire door locked at the top of the stairs from the Melody Lounge

2 Concealed and locked double doors to Shawmut Street

3 Shawmut Street exit door

4 Locked backstage exit door

5 Locked performers' entrance to stairs to second-floor dressing rooms

6 Stairway up to performers' dressing rooms

7 Inward-opening door to New Lounge vestibule

Approximate scale

0   30 feet

and realized that the club was on fire. She could see the door on the Shawmut Street side and tried to cross the dining room to get to it. Someone knocked her to the ground, and before she could get up, an overturned table hit her squarely in the face. She blanked out and came to with the pressure of feet on her body, the heavy tread of men and the stabbing impact of high-heel shoes. She heard moans, shrieks, and someone calling, "Mother . . . Mother . . . Mother." She herself was praying as she reached up and touched a man's hand and found herself yanked to her feet, her gown completely torn away. That was a blessing: she could see women, as bright as torches, as their evening gowns burst into flames. She tried to follow the man who pulled her up but he plunged ahead in the swirling mass of people. She pushed forward and fell into a sea of people; they piled on top of her. She could feel the skin on her arms burning as if they were splashed with acid, and then she didn't feel anything at all.

Joseph F. Kelley, a building contractor, his friend Benjamin Wheaton, and Wheaton's wife were having drinks at the Caricature Bar when Kelley heard a commotion and figured a fight had broken out. Then Wheaton said quietly to his wife, "It's a fire," and the three headed toward the passageway into the Broadway Lounge. As panicked people blocked the way, Kelley was knocked down and lost sight of the Wheatons. He made his way through the passageway in the new lounge as the thick and oily smoke grew heavy and the lights went out. As Kelley later told police, "I felt a body. It was a girl. I picked her up. There was a strata of air under the smoke. You could see ahead [where] the tables had been all knocked over the stools. We picked our way over the stools. The crowd at the door pushed us out."

Even as the main dining room was erupting in chaos, drinking continued in the Broadway Lounge. Mixing drinks was bartender William "Tiny" Shea, who topped the scales at 385 pounds. James Welansky, Barnett's brother, was sharing a table with Boston police night captain James Buccigross, who was supposedly making his nightly rounds, and Suffolk County assistant district attorney Garrett Byrne. With Barnett in the hospital, James Welansky was there, as he later told investigators, "to look out for his [brother's] interests." As the reputed gangster shared a drink and conversation with the two Boston officials, a hostess ran up to tell him the main dining room was on fire. Barely had the words left her mouth when smoke started to pour into the lounge, followed by a rush of people who had managed to navigate the passageway from the dining room. Captain Buccigross attempted to call for order; he was knocked aside. Somehow both he and James Welansky managed to reach the doors leading out of the lounge. Of the two doors into the lounge, an inside vestibule door opened inward, against the flow of human traffic bearing down on it. The crowd pushed the door shut and the crush kept it shut. Others helplessly beat on the lounge's thick glass windows as the room filled with flames and smoke.

Other Cocoanut Grove staff, despite the panic, attempted to get as many people out as possible. Head waiter Frank Balzarini heroically directed people, refusing to leave, until he succumbed to the smoke. In the second floor of the two-story building that housed the Broadway Lounge, the show dancers and chorus girls—who had been waiting for the second show—were alerted to the fire when a waiter found his way upstairs to the second-floor dressing rooms and told them to climb out the window onto the roof of the adjoining building, which housed the main dining room. Several dancers climbed out into the freezing cold; dance captain Jackie Maver led others, including Henrietta Siegel (known professionally as Pepper Russell), down the stairway, now dark and filled with smoke. They inched their way and managed to find an open door. Other dancers jumped from the roof or were rescued by firefighters.

From the stage, bass player Lesberg could see the commotion in the foyer, followed by fast-moving flames. Lesberg hesitated; he didn't want to leave his new, precious bass, but soon the entire band was fleeing the stage. A drummer refused to leave until, with help, his drums were yanked from the stage. Lesberg grabbed his bass and joined the stampede, only to find himself stalled in a small room behind the stage, which led downstairs to a back door. As the lights went out, the room filled with smoke and the basement door appeared to be locked. Lesberg dropped his bass; jammed in with about fifty others, including Fazioli and Willet, he couldn't move. Willet pulled out a handkerchief and pressed it to his mouth. "I guess this is it," he said to Lesberg, before they both sagged to the floor. Lesberg was curiously without fear; everything was becoming hazy and he passed out onto a growing pile of bodies.

Meanwhile, crouched behind the Melody Lounge bar, Weiss slowly realized that the fire seemed to be gone. The lounge was totally quiet, although filled with smoke and a strange pungent odor. He rose and, tripping over bodies, stumbled into the kitchen where, to his astonishment, a group of people huddled. Among them was head cashier Katherine Swett, determined not to leave the club's money unguarded. Now certain he knew a way out, Weiss convinced the group to follow him through the basement furnace room to a service door. But the sight of the furnace's lights and the heat spooked the group and they ran back into the kitchen. Weiss tried to argue, but they said they'd stay put and wait for firemen. Weiss promised to send help and dashed through the furnace room. In the searing heat, he found an open service exit and escaped into the cold air. The party he had tried to lead out was later found dead in the kitchen. Weiss could do nothing more than help pull out bodies; he helped bring out more than twenty before he collapsed around twelve-thirty in the morning.

Bedlam on the streets, the night of the fire. (Courtesy of the **Boston Herald***)*

The basement proved to be a better escape route than the upstairs. Some people got out of the club by crawling through a small basement window into a small courtyard. Busboy Tony Marra found clean air by opening a freezer and sticking his head into an empty ice-cream bucket. Then he heard a clang, and he raced to the walk-in refrigerator, where about fifteen people had crammed themselves in. He pounded on the door, screaming: "Please let me in, I'm only fifteen years old." He heard only, "Get out of here, kid, there's no room left." Marra dashed back into the kitchen, where he spotted a window between steam pipes and, smashing the glass, wiggled to safety, maple walnut ice cream dripping from his hair.

The streets outside the club had turned into bedlam—a mix of the living and the dead, rescue workers and firefighters. Some who managed to get out walked a few steps and collapsed as the cold air hit their lungs. Victims screamed for help, husbands screamed for wives, and friends were frantically searching for friends. When singer Billy Payne got out, "My reaction was to lose everything in my stomach. . . . I met Mickey Alpert with a woman's white coat on and he hugged me." People coming out of other nightclubs and movie theaters pitched in, including thirty-three-year-old lawyer Frank Shapiro. Coming out of the Metropolitan Theatre with his wife, he saw the smoke and heard the fire engines. He sent his wife home and ran over to help, dragging bodies, living and dead, from the club's doors and laying them on the sidewalk. He later learned that a cousin, medical student Joseph Dreyfus, was caught in the fire. A few would-be rescuers tried to get inside the club, among them Gloucester sailor Stanley Viator, who had been passing through the area when the fire broke out. He repeatedly dashed into the club to pull out patrons; on his fourth trip, he did not come out. Jackie Maver's boyfriend, navy seaman Albert Drolette, ran to the Grove when he heard of the fire, not realizing his girlfriend had made it out—he charged into the building only to become trapped inside. He was rescued when someone saw his hand moving in a pile of bodies—he was badly injured but recovered. Navy seaman Howard E. Sotherden of Tiverton, Rhode Island, in Boston on a two-day pass, braved the choking smoke to pull out four people: two dead, two alive. As he pulled out one man, whose glasses still hung from one ear, he heard someone say in astonishment, "Hey, that's Marty Sheridan."

Of all the heroes of the day, few were more brave—and tragic—than coastguardsman Clifford Johnson. The Missouri resident had managed to escape the fire without injury. But he returned time and time again, trying to find his date. On his fourth trip out, he exited in a ball of flames. He was rushed to Boston City Hospital with second- and third-degree burns over 75 percent of his body. Nurses stripping the uniform from his body could not tell where the cloth ended and charred flesh began. The burns were so deep that two of his ribs were exposed, and nurses could not find an unburned spot on his body to take his blood pressure. Yet, while in deep shock, he was alive. The staff figured all they could do would be to ease him into death.

The fire's speed and ferocity still baffle fire analysts. In a summary often repeated in subsequent histories, Paul Benzaquin, in his 1959 book on the fire, declared, "Twelve minutes after the tree caught fire, everyone who was to die was dead or mortally burned." According to the best estimates, flames broke out in the Melody Lounge at about 10:15 P.M. Within a minute the fire had spread to the foyer upstairs. By 10:18, the main dining area was embroiled. Two minutes later, fire raced through the passageway into the Broadway Lounge. By 10:35 the first victim arrived at Boston City Hospital. And by 10:45, firefighters had the main body of the fire under control. Of the strange coincidences of the fire, none was stranger than the minor fire that brought firefighters only blocks from the Cocoanut Grove just as the Melody Lounge was going up in flames.

CHAPTER FOUR

Fighting the Blaze

At 10:15 P.M. on November 28, Boston's fire department received an alarm from box number 1514 in the theater district; a passerby wanted to report a car on fire at the corner of Stuart and Carver streets, just blocks from the Cocoanut Grove. Because that alarm box was in a high-density area, a large contingent of firefighters and apparatus responded: four engine companies, two ladder companies, and one rescue company, accompanied by deputy chief Louis Stickel and district chief Daniel Crowley. Engine Company No. 22, first on the scene, extinguished the car fire within a minute. Lieutenant Miles Murphy and Charles Kenney of Rescue One, Captain Jeremiah Cronin and George "Red" Graney of Engine Company No. 35, and other men used this as a chance to chat. As they were unhurriedly putting away their equipment, they heard a commotion and thought that a fight—probably between a couple of sailors—had broken out at the nearby Cocoanut Grove. Then, "Hey, there's another fire!" someone shouted, and the firefighters saw trails of smoke. Almost at that moment someone pulled fire alarm box 1521 at Church and Winchester streets, and the wife of an off-duty fireman, who had already rushed downstairs, was telephoning to report that she could see smoke at the Cocoanut Grove from her second-story window. Members of Engine Company 22 revved their engine and quickly drove in the direction of the fire. Pulling up near the corner of Broadway and Shawmut streets, they heard screaming and saw people running from the club and flames roaring out of the door of the Broadway Lounge. Jumping from their rig, the men started dragging a hose toward the Broadway door to get water into the new lounge. Firefighters could also see flames pouring from the Shawmut Street door as people with their hair and clothes on fire stumbled from the club.

As Lieutenant Murphy focused on the Broadway side of the club, firefighter Kenney ran to the Shawmut Street door. He could see what looked like a growing pile of bodies inside. "Get a line to play in the door!" Kenney yelled. He didn't wait for the water; he plunged into the building, desperate to get out some of those people. Meanwhile, as water played over the Broadway door, firefighters from Ladder Company No. 13 tried to smash the glass block windows to get to people inside; the modern windows resisted the fiercest blows. When the men finally broke through, they could see burning, blackened hands reaching for help that was coming too late.

Told by District Chief Crowley that people were trapped inside, deputy chief Louis Stickel skipped the second alarm and ordered a third. It went out at 10:23; a fourth alarm followed at 10:24. Eventually, twenty-five Boston engine companies, five ladder companies, one water tower, and three rescue companies came to the scene. Some fire companies, arriving at the Piedmont Street side of the club, were momentarily unaware of the drama around the corner on Broadway. Flames were shooting twenty feet out from the main entrance; peering through the arches, firefighters could see the panicked pileup at the revolving door. When they finally smashed the front walls and windows, they were driven back by intense heat and flames. All they could do was pour water into the entryway and watch helplessly as many people burned to death. Firefighters fruitlessly tried to break down the door that led to the staircase to the Melody Lounge—the door that was supposedly equipped with a panic bar. Only with a battering ram were they able to smash the door open. Inside they found dozens of bodies.

On Shawmut Street, Graney managed to get a charged, high-pressure hose inside the main dining room. Amid the flames and gushing water, Kenney and other firefighters pulled people and bodies from the club, their hands blackened by heat from the victims' charred

Trying to assist victims, as bodies piled up outside the nightclub. (Courtesy of the **Boston Herald***)*

flesh. Firemen smashed the windows on Shawmut and broke through the thin wood panels, trying to vent the fire and provide more exits. Kenney saw, in a pile of bodies, a woman's small hand desperately waving. "Hold on, sister, hold on," he cried and firmly grabbed her wrist, even though he could feel his fingers sinking down through burned flesh to bone. "Take it easy. We'll get you out of there in a minute." He could feel her hand grabbing his, grabbing with all her strength. He managed to pull the woman to her feet. Her clothes were torn away and she was badly burned, but Dotty Myles was carried out alive. Kenney continued his rescue work until he collapsed and was taken to a hospital. Doctors later found claw marks on his legs, evidence of the frantic appeals of dying club patrons.

So many bodies were being pulled out of the club that rescue workers were forced to make terrible decisions, trying to determine those who were still breathing and get them into transport, and piling the corpses like cordwood on the sidewalk. A priest moved among the crowd administering last rites. Buck Jones, recognized by his fine cowboy boots, was carried out. The injured were hustled into any available

29

transportation—police cars, taxis, dump trucks—even passing motorists were stopped and their vehicles turned into makeshift ambulances. Dotty Myles sat dazed on the sidewalk; apparently no one thought she would live. Gathering her strength she leaped into an ambulance already packed with victims. When it reached Boston City Hospital, she was the only one alive.

The eighteen streams of water that firefighters poured into the club began to bring the flames under control. Aerial ladders went up on the Broadway and Shawmut side; the chorus girls who sought refuge on the roof were helped out; and firefighters scrambled onto the roof to vent the fire and provide access for hoses. An attempt was made to open the rolling roof to vent the blaze but the fuse had been removed to prevent drunken pranks. As interviewed decades later by fire researcher Casey C. Grant, "Red" Graney said he tried to get inside the Broadway Lounge and found himself looking into the eyes of a young woman yelling, "Please get me out, my father will be worried." The fire drove him back, but he pressed in with the hose to reach the girl, climbing painfully over what seemed like mountains of bodies, and other rescuers helped the girl to safety.

When fireman John Collins made his way into the dining room, the smell of burned flesh was overwhelming. Yet some bodies seemed to be hardly burned at all; there were only slight smudges under their noses. Inside the Melody Lounge, he saw, to his astonishment, a very pretty girl sitting at the table with her eyes open and her hand on a cocktail glass. Collins couldn't figure out why she was just sitting here; walking up to her, he realized she was dead.

Among the firefighters was twenty-seven-year-old John F. Crowley of Engine Company No. 9, working his very first shift as a Boston firefighter. As Engine 9 pulled up to the scene, Crowley heard the command: "Run a line from their pump to the doorway on Shawmut Street and get water into the building." As Crowley carried his part of the hose, he passed men and women staggering in a daze, babbling deliriously. He saw others sprawled on the sidewalk, horrifyingly still. Just concentrate on the job, his instincts told him. He and his crew dragged the hose inside the door; bodies were piled shoulder high on each side, creating an eerie passageway. As the firemen fumbled in the dark, suddenly the lights came on and the full impact hit Crowley. He saw people still sitting at tables; they had died without even moving. He could see another pile of bodies between the Caricature Bar and what seemed to be a long window. A horrified Crowley realized that the fancy drapery over the window had burned off, revealing light from the lamppost outside; people had seen this light and had thrown themselves over the bar trying to get out. They didn't know that an iron grill covered the outside of the window. They had no chance of escape and died in the smoke and heat.

Although Crowley's company was ready with water, it was not needed. By 10:45 P.M. the fire was out. The firefighters now had to try to find the living and to retrieve the dead. This was an even more devastating task than fighting the fire, as some bodies were in burned pieces. As he walked out of the dining room, Crowley saw $1, $2, $5, and $10 bills scattered over the floor. How little money meant now, he thought.

CHAPTER FIVE

Medical Breakthroughs

Boston City Hospital nurses and doctors were getting a jump on Christmas the night of November 28; many of the staff—even those off duty—were at the hospital for a holiday party. Most were still celebrating when the first victims of the fire—three men whose hands and faces were covered with first- and second-degree burns—ran into the emergency room. More victims started coming in—by ambulance, by private car, by taxi, and even firetruck. The staff, now realizing a major disaster was in full swing, dived into work; the extra help from partygoers was invaluable for the terrible nights and days to follow. Soon, a patient was arriving every eleven seconds, which, according to the December 9, 1942, *Boston Traveler*, was "a rate speedier than any ever established by a hospital during London's worst air raids." About three hundred people were taken to Boston City Hospital; only 131 survived the first few hours.

At Boston City Hospital that night was Dr. Stanley Levenson, a recent medical school graduate studying burn treatment. But he was neither on duty nor at the party—he was hospitalized with acute gastroenteritis. When victims started arriving, he was told to get to the emergency room. Choking back nausea from the smell of burned flesh and smoke, Levenson went to work. His first job was to distinguish the living from the dead. Sixty years later, he told medical writer Barbara Ravage that he never returned to his hospital bed but for the next three days did nonstop rounds twenty-four hours a day.

Across town at Massachusetts General Hospital, Dr. Francis Moore, a resident on call, listened to a football game and chatted with his colleagues. At about ten thirty that night the whines of the first ambulances drifted in above the announcer's voice. Moore paid no attention at first. But the sirens went on and on, and Moore donned his white coat and ran toward the emergency room. The full impact of the disaster struck him as he got to the hall outside the ER—the air was rank with the smell of burnt clothes and hair and already dead bodies were being lined up in the hall. MGH had received 114 patients; within hours only 39 were alive.

Doctors and nurses were confronted with a bewildering mix of injuries. Many victims were horribly burned, skin curling from their knuckles and arms, their faces already bloating from the terrible heat. Some faces were a deceptively healthy bright red—a sign of carbon monoxide poisoning. Other faces were pale and waxen, the lips blue, an indication that oxygen had been stripped from their blood. Some victims were coughing and vomiting black-tinged mucus. Moore could see frothy pink secretions on some lips—a condition observed in soldiers poisoned by mustard gas in World War I. Burns, horrible as they were, were overshadowed by respiratory problems. About 107 of the 131 initial survivors at Boston City Hospital and 36 of the 39 at MGH suffered some kind of lung damage.

Contrary to mythology of panic, relatively few patients suffered from broken limbs caused by the mad panic to exit. MGH staffers found no fractures and only slight trauma to soft parts; William Watters, associate medical examiner for Southern Suffolk County, later reported that he found only one broken rib. While many patients were obviously injured in the panic, the life-threatening injuries came from the fire and smoke.

By fortunate timing, area hospitals had prepared and rehearsed wartime disaster plans; MGH had also conducted two research projects on burn treatment. Now both preparedness and research were put to the test. Staff administered oxygen, fluids, and blood plasma; patients given morphine were marked with a red grease-pencil M on their forehead or chest. For the next forty-eight hours, nurses and doctors around the city—other Boston-area hospitals also received a smattering of Grove victims—did not sleep. Their challenges were gruesome. Many patients howled with agony or behaved bizarrely, the result of shock and horror. As he described in a letter to his parents (published in the *New Yorker* on May 5, 2003), Dr. Moore saw a young girl

> *with her clothing burned off, and her skin hanging like ribbons as she flailed her arms around, screaming with pain. Another, a naval lieutenant who kept repeating over and over again, 'I must find her. I must find her.' His face and hands were the dead paper-white that only a deep third-degree burn can be, and I knew only looking at him for a moment that if he lived, in two weeks his face would be a red, unrecognizable slough. He didn't live.*

Boston City Hospital staff tried to help patients who were stirring restlessly or shaking with chills and nausea. Even those who arrived at the hospital with minimal burns began to have difficulty breathing, their coughing and wheezing becoming severe as swelling blocked their breathing passages. "I feel like I'm being choked," many gasped to nurses. Doctors and nurses struggled to control their own gagging at the smell of smoke and the pungent odor of charred flesh, which intensified as they approached patients.

The first step at both hospitals was to separate the living from the dead. Eerily, some of the dead bore no marks at all, no burns, no discoloring, their eyes closed as if asleep, with only dark smudges under their noses. To Thomas Coleman, a second-year medical student at MGH, the red faces seemed simply bright with the "blush of youth." For a fleeting moment, he smelt the fragrance of gardenias—perhaps from corsages. It seemed impossible that these bright souls, silent, still beautiful, would never wake up. "But their flowers aren't burned!" he cried. At Boston City Hospital, staffers found, to their horror, one of their own, an intern. He was thought to be among the dead when he gasped. Even after vigorous and prolonged artificial respiration and stimulation, he remained comatose and died thirty hours later.

The standard treatment for burns at that time was to remove dead and decaying tissue and blisters from the burned skin (a procedure called debridement) and apply tannic acid to create a leathery scab that would seal the wound and prevent infection. In another recent innovation, burns were sprayed with a mixture of textile dyes called "triple dye" or with silver nitrate to seal the wound. At Boston City Hospital, burns were sprayed with the triple dye combination or with tannic acid and silver nitrate. Dr. Oliver Cope, then a promising researcher at MGH and later president of the American Surgical Association, wanted to try another approach; he believed body fluid loss and internal infection posed a greater immediate danger than skin damage, and thus treatment of shock and other internal problems was initially just as—if not more—important than treating the actual burns. He had been researching a new kind of treatment in which burns were wrapped with a fine mesh gauze impregnated with a petroleum jelly and boric acid mixture, and intensive intravenous fluids were administered. Cope and his colleague Dr. Bradford Cannon tried the process on a large scale, aided by residents such as Dr. Moore. As burn victims came in, sterile towels were placed over their wounds; when a patient was settled, the burn surfaces were covered with the boric-impregnated gauze. The burns were neither cleansed nor debrided, and the dressings were not changed until the fifth or tenth day. The results, as Cope later put it, were "gratifying." Second-degree wounds healed with minimal scarring, and deeper burns were free of invasive infection. After Cope and Cannon published their results in the *Annals of Surgery* in 1943, doctors began to change procedures for treating burns, shifting to the "softer" petroleum jelly and boric acid approach. "The advantage," Cope noted, "lies in its simplicity."

Even if burns were successfully treated, patients were in grave danger from infection. Many were given sulfadiazine, a relatively new class of agents aimed at controlling lethal blood infections. But an urgent request went out for a brand-new substance that seemed miraculous in its ability to halt infection: penicillin. The mold-produced agent was then considered a highly guarded secret and used only for the military; it was in very short supply. But thirty-two liters of the drug in culture liquid form were rushed to MGH from New Jersey in a few days. Because penicillin was administered in very low doses, its efficacy could not be clearly established. But publicity about this new "miracle" drug convinced the previously skeptical American pharmaceutical industry to start producing mass quantities of the agent. It was the beginning of the age of antibiotics.

Even with medical innovations, many patients simply could not recover from their massive wounds. Dr. Thomas Risley, a surgical intern at MGH, was assigned to treat the badly injured Buck Jones. As the cowboy's neck swelled, his breathing tube was blocked and Risley and another resident spent more than two hours trying to locate his trachea for a tracheotomy. The tough hombre lingered for two days before dying from his wounds. In the critical need for blood, hospital staff lined up to donate. Others stood outside on the street, pulling in passersby on foot and in cars, begging for help. Boston citizens responded; twelve hundred gave blood within days. The trauma, however, went on for weeks as patients, despite valiant efforts by doctors, succumbed to injuries. Of three Boston City Hospital patients with burns over 30 percent of their bodies, one died in four hours, one in twenty-eight days, and another nearly six months later. Doctors at both hospitals were puzzled by what had caused extensive lung injuries, including distinct respiratory lesions. Generally, the more severely burned patients had the most severe lung problems—but a significant minority of patients who had minimal or no burns had severe and even fatal respiratory lesions. Dr. Levenson was among the doctors mystified by the wholesale destruction in lower airways, below the vocal cords, and the unusual lesions in the lungs; he initially suspected that the fire had released a pulmonary irritant, phosgene, possibly as a product of burning Freon, a common refrigerant coolant. Other experts and witnesses insisted that the nightclub smoke wasn't just ordinary smoke. "Many of the victims had the appearance of soldiers I saw gassed in the First World War," William J. Brickley, medical examiner for Northern Suffolk County, testified in hearings after the fire. Medical examiner Timothy Leary of Southern Suffolk testified, "There is no question, however, but what there was something poisonous beside carbon monoxide in that smoke." Newspapers buzzed with speculation about the "mystery gas," but the exact properties could not be determined.

The "mystery gas" puzzled Boston for months. Dr. Levenson later concluded that the severe lung damage was caused not by phosgene but by the chemicals in smoke, ranging from carbon monoxide to hydrogen cyanide, ordinarily produced when wood, paper, and textiles were partially burned. Those who managed to cover their faces with a damp cloth—like bartender Daniel Weiss and singer Billy Payne—managed to escape with little damage. Those who passed out and continued to breathe smoke suffered the worst damage.

Three years after the fire, however, Harvard Medical School researchers found that when the leatherette that covered the club's wall and furniture was subjected to extreme heat, it produced the potentially lethal fume acrolein, a substance found in tear gas. Acrolein may have been the "mystery gas" that caused lesions in the victims' lungs.

The fire also left wounds undetectable by any physical measurement. Thirty-year-old Francis Gatturna of Roslindale escaped the fire with minor burns, but his wife perished in the inferno. He was readmitted to Massachusetts General Hospital on January 1 when his worried family brought him back. The young man was restless and agitated and started conversations only to break them off abruptly. "Nobody can help me. When is it going to happen? I am doomed, am I not?" he would repeatedly utter. He obsessed about his wife's fate, explaining again and again that he had tried to pull her out but had fainted and was shoved out by the crowd. "I should have saved her or I should have died, too," he insisted. After five days in which staff and doctors tried to assuage his guilt, Gatturna began to calm down. On the sixth day, after skillfully distracting the attention of his special nurse, he jumped out a window to his death.

Gatturna's mental trauma was not unique. Other fire victims reported getting panic attacks in restaurants; those more severely burned felt disfigured, with no chance at future happiness. Doctors Stanley Cobb and Erich Lindemann conducted a landmark study of Cocoanut Grove victims, one of the nation's first attempts to examine the issue of survivor's guilt and the aftereffects of trauma, the beginning of the era in which victims of violence or trauma were no longer told just to get over it. "It seems that the grieving person can delay his grieving period but not avoid it and that individuals who show no signs of grief during the period of convalescence from their somatic injuries are likely to have disabling disturbances at a later period," they concluded.

For Boston, the grieving would go on for years, without closure or resolution.

CHAPTER SIX

The Aftermath, Investigation, and Trial

Headlines in Boston newspapers on November 29 and thereafter screamed with horror and confusion. "400 Dead in Hub Night Club Fire, Hundreds Hurt in Panic as Cocoanut Grove Becomes Wild Inferno," the *Globe* declared. Cried the *Herald*: "450 Die as Flames and Panic Trap Cocoanut Grove Crowd, Scores of Service Men are Lost, Fire Worst in City's History, Few Victims Identified." The *Boston Advertiser*: "399 Dead, 200 Injured in Cocoanut Grove Fire: Scores Held in Trap by Wild Panic." The death and injury toll would not be established for weeks; indeed, in many ways, it has never been sorted out. Estimates ranged wildly in the days after the fire and through the weeks to come as bodies were counted and re-counted and the injured died of their wounds.

The identification of the badly burned dead presented particular trauma for families and friends; news photos captured the grim stoicism of mothers and fathers lined up outside mortuaries or waiting in the facilities' amphitheaters—some holding out hope that they would not find a loved face among the charred bodies. About two hundred people had died trying to escape through the revolving door; another hundred had died in the Broadway Lounge; at least twenty-five or thirty bodies were found piled behind the bolted exit door on Piedmont Street; other bodies were found throughout the complex. At least 170 people were seriously injured. The final death toll is now generally accepted as 492; the last person to die from wounds suffered in the fire succumbed in May 1943 (after the manslaughter trial on the fire had been concluded); and Francis Gatturna, the man who killed himself after surviving the fire, has been deemed among the casualties.

Sheer numbers do not reflect the impact on Boston, Worcester, and other communities. Dead were the newlyweds John and Claudia

Identifying the dead at the Southern Mortuary. (Courtesy of the **Boston Herald***)*

O'Neill, with their best man and the maid of honor, the groom's sister. Only their photo, snapped by Grove photographer Lynn Andrews, survived. All four sons of seventy-one-year-old widow Mary Fitzgerald were dead. The "football" crowd included a party of seven—members of the Whitmarsh family. The three young Whitmarsh children lost their father, mother, grandfather, grandmother, and two aunts. About fifty-one servicemen and two WAVEs were dead. Of Buck Jones's party, nearly half were dead. Buck Jones's Junior Commandos, some of whom had just met their hero, were heartbroken. "There were solemn little services of about 3 minutes each held in attics, cellars, barns, churches, schools, front verandas, huts and rooms in the family home," wrote Paul Waitt, the area commando-in-chief, in the December 4 *Boston Traveler*.

The nightclub's staff was decimated. Katherine Swett, the cashier who refused to leave her post, was found dead beside the untouched cash box. Headwaiter Frank Balzarini had died in his effort to guide patrons out of the club. The singer Grace Vaughn (real name Grace McDermott) was dead; reportedly, she had calmly announced to the patrons in the Broadway Lounge that the club was on fire and they should leave. She then dutifully returned to her post—her piano. Maxine Coleman, a beloved buxom, rowdy singer, was also dead. Broadway Lounge bartender "Tiny" Shea fought for his life. He had seen dark gray fumes rush into the lounge, and after inhaling the "strong and bitter smoke" he had covered his face with a wet bar rag. As he struggled to the exit, he was tripped by the stampede, falling face down. His clothes caught fire and his back and shoulders burned—more than 30 percent of his body. Boston City Hospital staff attempted to save him by immobilizing his burned body with his face down. He pleaded with doctors to turn him over. "Please get me off my stomach," he cried repeatedly, as nurses gently tried to explain that he needed to remain in that position. After twelve weeks of agony, Shea succumbed.

Jack Lesberg found himself regaining consciousness in Boston City Hospital. Dawn had not yet arrived but he could feel the pandemonium everywhere. He realized that a nearby priest was preparing to give him last rites. "Just a minute," he croaked, as he struggled to open his eyes. A doctor grabbed the priest and they moved to someone else. Bandleader Bernie Fazioli had been rescued along with Lesberg but died of his injuries. Saxophonist Romeo Ferrara (who saw himself erroneously listed as dead) and drummer Al Maglitta survived. Al Willet was nowhere to be found. His girlfriend, Henrietta Siegel, the dancer who escaped with Jackie Maver, searched for him through the night, but he was not in the hospital. She hoped that perhaps he had gone home. As morning approached, she forced herself to go to the Southern Mortuary. As a priest tried to comfort her there, they heard a groan from a "body." It was Al. He had been mistakenly transported among the corpses to the mortuary. He would survive.

Death notices and accounts of funerals filled entire pages of the *Herald* and *Record American*. On December 3 alone, 150 funerals were scheduled. The chapel bell at Malden's Holy Cross Cemetery tolled almost continuously, as nineteen burials were scheduled. Outrage replaced shock, and Boston officials suspended the entertainment permits of 35 hotels and 682 restaurants and taverns.

The day after the fire, Boston fire commissioner William Arthur Reilly opened an investigation as the city cried out for answers: How did this happen in the Athens of America? The Reilly hearings continued until January 20, 1943, bringing forth more than two hundred witnesses, with horrific, often contradictory, stories. Mickey Alpert, Daniel Weiss, Benjamin Wheaton, and John Bradley spoke of their escapes, while Boston building inspector Theodore Eldracher, decorator Reuben Bodenhorn, and Lieutenant Frank Linney described conditions at the club. As reporters scribbled notes, Jean Termin of the North End said that she had seen a club employee "stand in front of the door—hold out his arms—and tell people that all bills must be paid before leaving." Maurice Levy told of watching the busboy light the match in the Melody Lounge and how he lost his wife in the stampede to the revolving door. Others described the panic amid the maelstrom of heat and smoke. It was a litany of the lucky, the stories of those who lived to talk.

Joseph F. Kelley, the building contractor, spoke clearly and precisely. The fire "was bluish with a yellow cast as if something were burning in suspension. It wasn't burning at any particular point. The air was full of flame yet the walls and ceiling were not then on fire," he testified. As the ball of fire passed from the foyer into the dining room, it "leveled out on the ceiling. The flames passed over my head in the passageway and went into the new lounge." Asked to describe the smoke's odor, Kelley said,

"It was like nothing I have ever known. I have had a rasping feeling in my throat and chest and food hasn't tasted the same." His companion Benjamin Wheaton described seeing smoke that "rolled up as a wave would roll in from the ocean."

With brother Barnett still hospitalized, James Welansky gave vague, even sullen responses to Reilly's questions. Asked who took care of fire-proofing decorations in the club, he replied, "The decorators. I don't know too much about those things. I'm just giving you my supposition." He testified that he didn't know exactly how he got out: "I seemed to be pushed along and carried out." He also avowed that the two doors to the Broadway Lounge opened outward—a blatant lie— and that the club was "crowded but not overcrowded."

The Reilly witnesses gave Boston a glimpse into the heart of the inferno. The normally ebullient Mickey Alpert, his hands bandaged and his face haggard, gave a dazed and confusing story. Alpert had been discovered outside the club by civil defense director John Walsh. The former master of ceremonies said that after he realized there was a fire, not a fight, he tried to get out through a service door behind the stage; it was locked, then people pushed it open. He talked about opening another door only to find flames behind it. He also recalled breaking bars on a downstairs window and pushing people through. Then he was trying to make it up the stairs but "I gave up. I said, 'This is it.' The next thing I know John Walsh is smacking me in the kisser."

Perhaps the most sensational testimony came from Charlestown sign maker Henry Weene, who testified that he had warned Barnett Welansky that a master electrician should be engaged to do the wiring in the new Broadway Lounge. "Welansky said it was not necessary because 'Mayor Tobin and I fit,'" Weene told investigators. He said he told Welansky, "That doesn't cover me much." Many seized on the oddly phrased comment as evidence of the complicity of higher-ups in helping the Cocoanut Grove management cover up negligence. Tobin himself first ignored Weene's testimony, but as the outrage increased, he issued a statement saying that Welansky had no right to make such an assertion "any more than any other man in business has a right to make any other similar statement with regard to me."

Other revelations about the club's furnishings and electrical wiring followed. The Boston Police Department archives contain a chilling

December 2, 1942, transcript of the questioning of Raymond Baer, an unlicensed electrician who had installed electrical fixtures in the Broadway Lounge without proper permits. Under questioning, Baer admitted that after he had been working at the club for six weeks, Welansky and contractor Samuel Rudnick talked "about no permit being on the job and Mr. Rudnick said it would all be taken care of." Pressed as to why he proceeded when he knew the work was illegal, Baer just repeated, "Things were said that everything was taken care of."

But things were not "taken care of." The club's wiring did not, to put it in legal terms, "conform to good practices." Bernard Welan, superintendent of the fire department's wiring division, told the Reilly commission that on November 7 and November 17 he had sent notices to the Cocoanut Grove warning that since the proper permits had not been obtained, the new lighting system was illegal.

The club's decorations were also suspected of causing or fueling the inferno. On December 2, state chemists announced that they had tested fifteen materials in the club, including fabric from the Melody Lounge, the fake palm tree leaves and wrapping, and the dining room's chairs and red imitation wall leather. Much of the material was highly flammable; the palm tree wrapping material, for example, "burst into violent flames instantly, in much the same manner as a dry Christmas tree." Fabric used in the club also ignited almost instantly and "was entirely consumed." Bodenhorn's fashionable leatherette covering burned quickly with "very irritating, acrid fumes." The palm tree leaves, surprisingly, showed the most resistance to flames, but the chemists concluded that the majority of the materials were not currently flame resistant, although they could not determine whether the materials had been treated in the past.

Even as city leaders vowed a full investigation of the tragedy, a sense of fatalism set in. Letters to newspapers seethed with rage and predicted that the tragedy would be swept under the rug, that the guilty would wiggle free. "Do 500 people have to be killed before they get out of their warm offices and do some investigating? In a small town everyone is afraid of the big shots," Phil Connell wrote to the *Boston Globe* a few days after the fire. "The Cocoanut Grove mass murder is the result of Boston's notoriously rotten politics," declared Eugene Willard in a December 14 letter to the *Globe*.

Investigating the fire. Although chemical tests on the leaves of the fake palm trees showed they were somewhat flame–resistant, many of the other club furnishings were found to be highly flammable. (Courtesy of the **Boston Herald***)*

Indeed, city officials were running for cover. "Three Boards Deny Responsibility" was the *Daily Record* headline three days after the fire, a day after the city's licensing board, the building department, and the Boston Police Department all said they had "no power to alter the condition of the building." The only person who appeared to be forthright about his involvement was young Stanley Tomaszewski, who told investigations he thought his match might have ignited the palm tree and set the club on fire. (Stanley's "forthrightness" was not immediate. See Chapter Seven.)

Even as he was conducting his investigation, Reilly found himself answering questions from state prosecutors who had convened a grand jury. Massachusetts attorney general Robert Bushnell kicked off a criminal investigation at the direction of governor Leverett Saltonstall. State fire marshal Stephen C. Garrity directed the effort; state police detective lieutenant Philip W. Deady was assigned as principal investigator. As the criminal investigation and the Reilly hearings continued, the rotten heart of Boston's number one glitter spot was gradually exposed. Investigators poking in the ruins found one of Welansky's secrets: a huge cache of more than four thousand cases of assorted liquor, lacking the government revenue tax seals. The liquor had been hidden in the ceiling behind a trap door; Welansky was apparently trying to dodge paying taxes on the booze. On December 11, investigators found a bricked-up door in the wall at the end of the Caricature Bar, an exit that would have provided an outlet to those caught on that side of the club. Welansky insisted it had been bricked up by the owner of a parking space outside who complained about club staff hanging around out there.

Local newspapers competed to find the latest developments. One reporter dug deep into the past to explain the present. Austen Lake, a scribe for the *Record American* with a jaunty, evocative style, had a way of injecting himself into his stories. He now focused his hard-edged energy on the Cocoanut Grove. He toured the wreckage of the building and helped produce one of the first diagrams of the complex. He claimed to establish "beyond question" that the interior hanging fabrics—which were supposed to be treated with flame retardant—were "not even remotely fireproof." Lake's tests were not exactly scientific: he helped himself to eight materials on the site, held a match to each, and subsequently reported that all "burned with an immediate, all-consuming intensity." More tellingly, Lake seized on the club's history as evidence that the fire was the inevitable consequence of corruption and greed. In a style long on flourish and somewhat stingy with facts, he wrote a multipart series on "The Rise and Fall of the Cocoanut Grove," which recounted the tale of Mickey Alpert, Jack Berman, King Solomon, and Welansky in a feverish rant, as if his information were personally transmitted by divine dictation.

For all his hyperbolic style, Lake hit a nerve. On December 14, the *Record* reported that Lake received threats and a phone call to "go easy" on the Cocoanut Grove; his editors (or Lake himself) wrote a defiant note, printed on December 16, replying that "you are hereby notified that on the contrary, Austen Lake will pull the lid off the situation in back of Cocoanut Grove." The threatening phone call had been traced and "we are ready for you." Such posturing might be dismissed as a paper-selling ploy, but the investigation had rattled someone. The lead state police investigator, Philip Deady, received death threats, and his son had to go to school under armed guard for a time.

Perhaps someone was worried about a box of unpaid food and liquor checks—signed off on by Grove management for the "right people"—that authorities confiscated on December 4. The bundle of meal and liquor checks included notations, such as "important," "a good friend," "see me," and "will settle later." Asked whose names were on the chits, a detective replied, "Names of some witnesses, you'll not ask us how to spell when you hear them." The box subsequently disappeared, Deady's son, Jack, recalled.

On December 31, 1942, the Welansky brothers and wine steward Jacob Goldfine were indicted on nineteen counts of involuntary manslaughter. Club designer Reuben Bodenhorn, Boston fire lieutenant Frank J. Linney—who had found conditions at the club "good"—Boston police captain Joseph Buccigross—who was in the club while he was supposed to be making his rounds—Boston building commissioner James Mooney, building inspector Theodore Eldracher, and contractors David Gilbert and Samuel Rudnick were indicted separately on charges ranging from conspiracy to violating building codes to willful neglect of duty.

The Welansky-Goldfine manslaughter trial lasted from March 15 to April 10, 1943. Attorney general Robert T. Bushnell brought the

Barnett Welansky (right), owner of the Cocoanut Grove. (Courtesy of Bill Noonan and the Boston Public Library)

charges in the name of nineteen victims, including Adele Dreyfus, arguing that the defendants caused the deaths by "willfully, wantonly and recklessly maintaining, managing, operating and supervising" the club. Wisely, the prosecution did not focus on the cause of the fire, which had not been officially determined; rather, they emphasized the unsafe conditions—the inadequate number of exits, the locked doors, the unlicensed electrical work, and the flammable furnishings. By the time the trial ended, 327 witnesses had testified and the jury had seen 131 exhibits, including a burned palm tree, the center post of the revolving door, and boxes of wires, carried in by state police lieutenant Deady.

Barnett Welansky's law partner, Herbert F. Callahan, defended him, and portrayed his client as a hardworking businessman who had no way of preventing the mad stampede in the inferno. Two other lawyers, Daniel Gallagher and Abraham C. Webber, defended Jacob Goldfine and James Welansky, who did not testify in their own defense. Barnett did, dissolving in tears on the stand, as Bushnell conducted a punishing cross-examination. Bushnell pushed the club owner hard over the question of why the exit door near the Melody Lounge was locked the night of the fire. Indeed a fireman had testified that he had to force the door open with an axe:

BUSHNELL: Whose responsibility was it to keep that door open for members of the public whom you invited to the Cocoanut Grove so that you should make money— whose responsibility was it?

WELANSKY: I told Balzarini [the head waiter who died in the fire] to keep that door open.

BUSHNELL: You knew there was a panic bolt on that door?

WELANSKY: Yes.

BUSHNELL: How did it happen that in addition to a panic lock there was a tongue lock on that door?

WELANSKY: I can't explain it. I don't know who did it.

Callahan, in summation, hammered on a lack of evidence: "There is no evidence that any one tried to use the Melody Lounge door. There is no evidence that Welansky ever ordered that the door be locked." Welansky, he said, could not have anticipated a conflagration, which started a mass stampede. Callahan insisted Welansky had never said anything about "Tobin and I fit" and sought to undercut Weene's credibility. The crux of Callahan's defense strategy, however, was that patrons caused their own death by panicking instead of exiting calmly: "You heard a witness say: 'It was every man for himself.' People were acting like wild animals. People were knocked down and trampled on. Many who did use their heads did get out. It was an occasion of terror, and once terror prevails, there is no telling what can happen." He continued, "Only yesterday you heard of five men sitting at a table with five women. The men tipped the table over on the women in their haste to escape. Once panic strikes, safety devices mean nothing at all. They are virtually useless."

Assistant district attorney Frederick T. Doyle gave the commonwealth's closing statement. According to reporters, Doyle "delivered his argument in a thunderous voice that gave spectators the impression he certainly was being heard down in Scollay Square." Barnett Welansky "rigged the whole situation," with Goldfine as his right-hand man and brother James in temporary control, Doyle told the jury. The club was, he said, "hermetically sealed." Patrons should have easily escaped via the panic lock in the Melody Lounge exit; instead "it was a phony. It was bolted."

Why was it kept locked? To keep some kid from slipping out without paying his check? We know it was locked. We know bodies were piled there. . . . To say this is an accident is ludicrous. Those responsible for that trap are sitting in the dock. . . . Someone said those who used their heads got out. James Welansky got out. Jacob Goldfine got out. But did the poor souls named here get out? It's a libel on the dead.

Doyle was relentless. "All day you have been filled up with smooth talk about panic. What did they expect the people to do? Stand up and be burned to death? They ran to one door. It was locked. They ran to another. It was locked. . . ."

Never mind about the busboy's match; greed caused the fire:

They were not content with an income of $1,000 a night. They blocked up an exit with a coat rack at a dime a head. There wasn't a penny to be lost. It was absolute greed and avarice. They were not content with the average flow of trade. Instead of advertising their "breathtaking" cocktail lounge, they should have advertised: "Come to the Grove and abandon hope."

In his nearly two-hour charge to the jury, judge Joseph L. Hurley warned that this case "is not an attempt to find someone on whom to pin the blame. It is not an attempt to find a scapegoat for public vengeance to be inflicted upon." Nor was it, he insisted, an investigation into the cause of the fire.

The jury was out for nearly five hours. They returned on April 10, 1943, with their verdict: Jacob Goldfine: Not guilty. James Welansky: Not guilty. Barnett Welansky: Guilty.

The verdict set a legal precedent for involuntary manslaughter caused through wanton or reckless conduct. While reckless conduct had generally involved an affirmative act, like driving a car, the Welansky case determined that reckless conduct, as distinguished from mere negligence, involved intentional failure to recognize potentially harmful conditions. On April 14, Judge Hurley sentenced an emotionless Welansky to twelve to fifteen years in prison, the "first 24 hours in solitary confinement and the residue at hard labor." Welansky was led away in manacles, the one person held responsible for so many problems. "It's too bad Barney has to take the rap," said Goldfine, and other employees agreed.

In other court action, in November 1943 Inspector Linney was acquitted of willful neglect of duty, and the following July charges were dropped against Buccigross. He was reinstated to duty, and eventually won back pay for the nineteen months he was suspended. Bodenhorn, Eldracher, and Gilbert were acquitted, and charges against building inspector James Mooney of conspiracy to violate building laws were dropped. Aside from Barnett Welansky, only contractor Samuel Rudnick was convicted; through legal maneuvering, his two-year jail sentence was indefinitely suspended.

If greed caused the Grove fire, greed continued to poison the lives of its victims. Money, jewelry, and personal items were looted from the bodies of victims, denying relatives mementos such as wedding rings and watches. More importantly, the club was found to be woefully underinsured. The six insurance companies involved paid out only $22,420 for damage to the club's contents; Welansky had not bothered to get liability insurance. The club building itself was deemed worthless. About five hundred injured and families of the dead filed some $8 million in damages against the club; some lawyers labeled the suits "outrageous." To sort out claims, prominent lawyer Lee M. Friedman was named receiver of the club; Friedman turned to a young associate, Frank H. Shapiro, the passerby who had pulled victims from the fire. Shapiro was instructed to drop all his cases, and for more than two years he worked on the nightclub case. It was, he recalled sixty-two years later, "a nightmare." The club's ownership—needed to establish liability—was a tangled web of documents, the club property itself was practically worthless, and the insurance payoff negligible. Moreover, Shapiro received threatening phone calls, telling him to keep his mouth shut about documents found at the club. "You're a nice young lawyer. You can live a nice long life," the voice on the phone sneered. He and his wife lived for a year under police guard.

The hidden cache of liquor was auctioned, with the intent that the $171,000 in proceeds go to victims. But the federal government, which had charged Welansky for tax evasion, demanded taxes be paid on the liquor as well as on the sale of the Grove land, as part of the Grove's assets. The government wanted $200,000—which would have left nothing for victims. After years of negotiation, the government reduced its claims by half, leaving $100,000 available for victims. In the end, survivors received only about $160 apiece for their pain and suffering, a "pittance," as Shapiro put it. The hospitals bore much of the treatment costs and the Red Cross pitched in with grants and other services. One of the tasks falling to the Red Cross was to reassure victims, many of whom were frantic about how they would pay for treatment, that they would get medical care.

The boarded, burned-out shell of the club, still attracting the curious, remained until 1945, when it was torn down. As workmen began to dismantle the building, they found eerie relics of the inferno—a wallet, an inscribed watch, a ticket stub to the Boston College–Holy Cross game, and sheet music for the song "My Last Affair." Then, even as the Grove disappeared, it yielded a last mystery.

Acting on a tip in June of 1945, police investigated the ruins and discovered that someone had entered the building and opened a safe hidden in a wall under the stairs to the Melody Lounge. Welansky claimed to know nothing about it, saying the safe must have been left over from the Solomon days. Waiting two and a half years, the burglars had torn out a large section of a wall leading to the safe, drilled it open, and vanished, leaving it empty. Its contents—if any—remain a mystery.

Barnett Welansky did not serve out his jail term. In 1946, dying from cancer, the former club owner was pardoned by Maurice Tobin, now the state's governor. Leaving prison, Welansky defended his release, saying, "If you were wrongfully convicted—framed—you'd feel you had a perfect right to be free." Tears came to his eyes and he added, "I only wish I had been at the fire and died with those others." He lived only another two months.

CHAPTER SEVEN

What Caused the Fire?

I t never became an issue at the trial, but the question would not go away: Did the busboy's match cause the fire? Initial witness accounts, including the busboy's own reckoning, would so indicate. And yet as soon as a few days after the fire, many began to question whether a single match could have caused such devastation. The question would haunt Stanley Tomaszewski for the rest of his life.

The sixteen-year-old Tomaszewski had managed to escape through the kitchen. He had remained at the Grove, helping to carry out victims and looking for his buddy who had helped get him the Grove job. The next morning, racked with guilt and shouldering responsibility that made him mature beyond his years, he went to police.

Fire historians have long hailed young Stanley as the one person willing to take responsibility about his role. His attitude won him support among police, investigators, and even Fire Commissioner Reilly. Yet Boston police records show that Tomaszewski was initially evasive about his actions in the Melody Lounge on the night of the fire. Four times, during his first interview with police on November 29, the day after the fire, police captain John F. McCarthy asked the boy point-blank: "Did you light a match?" Four times Tomaszewski replied, "No." Only when McCarthy asked the busboy if bartender John Bradley had told him to turn on the light in the palm tree did Tomaszewski open up.

He told me to put it on and I said to the party who was at the table, "You are not allowed to put out any lights. It is too dark." The party said jokingly, "Oh, leave it off." I couldn't see the bulb and I struck a match and put it on and then I stepped away. Then all of a sudden the palm tree seemed to take fire.

Pressed as to whether the match caused the fire, Stanley said defensively, "Well, it didn't start right away." McCarthy continued to push him: "So that, this fire started at the Cocoanut Grove, Stanley, as the result of your lighting a match?" "I believe so," the boy replied. A day later, when Fire Commissioner Reilly questioned him, Tomaszewski said that he had held onto the match until he got to the floor, when he stepped on it. When Reilly asked, "Do you think that match caught fire to the tree?" the boy replied, "It probably did."

Still, Reilly was impressed by the boy's manner. Authorities placed him in protective custody. A wise move, as family and friends of the victims were crying for vengeance, their grief spilling into anger. On Monday, "Police Say Busboy's Match Caused Fire" blazed across the front page of the *Boston Globe* as the city reeled in horror that one match could have caused such a holocaust. While crowds gathered outside the Tomaszewski home to denounce her son, Stanley's ailing mother cried over and over again to reporters, "Stanley is a good boy."

Within a week, doubts were raised about Stanley's match, no matter how straightforward his story seemed. "Busboy Did Not Start Fire: Hidden Blaze Raged in Walls" blared the *Boston Evening American* headline on December 7, 1942. Witness statements to the Reilly commission were confusing. Some said they did not see the match ignite the tree; rather they saw sparks *after* Stanley had already screwed in the lightbulb. Stanley himself thought he had carefully extinguished the match. Others described seeing a "flash." Some club goers told of being so hot in the lounge—the walls themselves seemed to radiate heat—that they decided to leave just before the fire broke out. A bit of the infamous palm tree in the Melody Lounge was, in fact, still intact—surely that would have been consumed first?

In his final report, Reilly absolved Tomaszewski of blame for the fire, writing: "After a careful study of all the evidence, and an analysis of all the facts presented before me, I am unable to find the conduct of this boy was the cause of the fire." He concluded: "This fire will be entered in the records of this department as being of unknown origin." State fire marshal Stephen Garrity also reached a similar roadblock. In a November 8, 1943, letter to governor Leverett Saltonstall, Garrity said that after examining Tomaszewki's testimony, "it is clear to me that he did not ignite the palm tree in the Melody Lounge and thereby cause the fire." In a separate report, Garrity echoed Reilly's conclusion: "After exhaustive study and careful consideration of all the evidence, and after many personal inspections of the premises, I am unable to find precisely and exactly the immediate cause of this fire."

Another great mystery was the fire's terrible speed. Could that have been caused by the flammable faux South Seas decorations, although they had supposedly been treated with flame retardant? Did the rapid

Despite the fast-moving ball of flame, many furnishings inside the Cocoanut Grove did not burn at all. (Courtesy of Bill Noonan)

burning of the furnishings create the fireball that many witnesses described? A large amount of the club's furnishings—chairs, bottles, bongo drums, even sheet music—remained unburned in the fire's rubble, baffling investigators. "Much of the cloth, rattan and bamboo contained in the Melody Lounge, and on the sides and lower walls of the stairway leading [from there], was, in fact, not burned at all and the same is true of carpet on the stairway, contrary to all usual fire experience," Reilly wrote in his extensive, sixty-four-page report on the fire issued on November 19, 1943. This indicates the fire did not "flashover," that is, reach the stage in which all exposed combustible material was burned.

Did faulty wiring cause the fire? Clearly, Welansky had cut corners by hiring unlicensed electricians. Lieutenant Philip Deady, the lead investigator for the state fire marshal's office, always harbored suspicions about the wiring, telling his son that

ignition was caused by a probable short circuit in the faulty, jerry-rigged wiring behind the false wall of the Melody Lounge, which caused a shower of sparks to escape through the air space between the false wall and true ceiling of the room onto the cotton "satin" ceiling covering. . . . This fabric burned with incredible rapidity, almost like an explosives fuse, involving the entire room in only a few minutes.

Contractor Joseph Kelley initially told police that, in his professional opinion,

It could have only been caused by a short circuit under the bar in the Melody Lounge. . . . In my opinion, a short circuit was spread down through and caused the wiring to set up spontaneous combustion. I never saw anything get going so sudden. There was so much smoke. But whatever happened, happened awfully fast.

That frightful speed, however, made many believe some kind of accelerant was at work. Said Reilly: "The substance of the fire was a highly-heated, partially burned but still burning, compressed volume of gas. By its nature this gas pressed for every available opening and I have found that this was the cause of its rapid course throughout the premises." The search for the mysterious accelerant—perhaps the same as the "mystery gas" that caused lung injuries—has inspired a range of theories, from the realistic to the outlandish. Gasoline fumes, from the club's days as a garage, had caught fire. Film stock, known to be flammable, might have still been on the premises. Reporter Austen Lake suggested that Nazi saboteurs, known to be operating on the East Coast, had set the fire; he didn't publish this theory, however, until 1964, which suggests that even this tabloid writer couldn't bring himself to believe it.

Robert Moulton, technical secretary of the safety committee of the National Fire Protection Association—an international nonprofit fire protection and prevention organization—wrote a detailed analysis of the fire published about a year after the tragedy. The fire "could have perhaps been started by defective amateur wiring to the fixture in the [palm] tree instead of by the [busboy's] match," he wrote. As for the cause of the fire's "incredible rapidity" and the mysterious lethal fumes, Moulton considered and rejected various theories, including those involving gasoline fumes or flammable motion picture film from the building's previous incarnations, as well as theories positing fumes caused by the large amount of alcohol being consumed, or by stored insecticide. "All the facts can perhaps be accounted for without seeking any mysterious or unusual explanation," Moulton concluded. "The combustible decorations, cloth finish on the ceiling and other readily combustible material could have caused a quick, hot and fast-spreading fire." Lung injuries "could be explained by the inhalation of ordinary smoke and superheated air."

Nearly thirty years later, in 1970, the Boston Fire Department again attempted to close the books on the fire. District fire chief John Vahey, a well-respected firefighter as well as historian, carefully re-examined the evidence, and, once again, found Tomaszewski's conduct blameless. He concluded that the department was still "unable to determine the original cause or causes of the fire." The busboy with the match remained the most logical explanation.

Following a commemoration of the fiftieth anniversary of the fire, another theory emerged. Two fire historians—firefighter Charles Kenney, son of firefighter Charles Kenney who rescued Dotty Myles at the fire, and Jack Deady, the son of investigator Philip Deady—have come to believe the initial accelerant was a refrigerant gas that raced through the club and ignited the furnishings. Moulton of the NFPA had ruled out refrigerator gas as an accelerant, saying none of the commonly used refrigerant gases were flammable or toxic. But in 1992, a retired refrigerator repairman, Walter Hixenbaugh, contacted Kenney. As a young man working with his father, Hixenbaugh had seen the club's refrigerator unit when it was removed from the club to his father's refrigerator service business in Cambridge, Massachusetts. Now living in Florida, Hixenbaugh told Kenney he was certain that the unit was not using Freon as a coolant, as Freon had been in short supply because of the war. The refrigerator used the gas methyl chloride. Hixenbaugh, who had been shipped overseas to fight in World War II, and so had missed the investigation into the fire and Welansky's trial, also remembered seeing small leaks in the unit's condenser tubing. Now he wrote to Kenney, wondering if the methyl chloride could explain the fire's rapid spread.

Interestingly, this was not the first time methyl chloride had been mentioned in connection with the Cocoanut Grove. Kenney found in the Boston Fire Department's archives a December 4, 1942, letter to reporter Austen Lake from W. Irving Russell, a radio and refrigerator serviceman. After reading Joseph Kelley's testimony during Reilly's hearings, Russell had written to Lake "in regard to the so called 'Mystery Gas'" to suggest that methyl chloride may have been substituted for Freon and that "a leak of this gas would produce conditions exactly as obtained in the Cocoanut Grove on the night of the fire." Lake, despite his vow to "blow the lid" off the Grove case, had not followed up on the tip.

Methyl chloride is, according to Frank L. Fire's "Hazardous Materials" notebook published in *Fire Engineering* in June 1989, "a flammable, toxic, corrosive, narcotic, clear, colorless gas with a sweet aroma similar to ether." It is usually stored and shipped as a liquid under pressure and "any liquid that is released will involve tremendous quantities of flammable, toxic, and corrosive gas." After talking with Hixenbaugh, Kenney came to believe that a refrigerator unit behind a wall in the Melody Lounge had in fact been supplied with methyl chloride, not Freon; the refrigerator unit leaked, the gas pooled and was ignited by an electrical spark, thus providing the accelerant that blew through the building and created the bluish flame Kelley described. This accelerant ignited the flammable fabric ceiling and the leatherette coverings, which burned rapidly and produced the "mystery gas" acrolein. Kenney argued that the floor plans of the club, made in December of 1942, showed a "fan compressor room" behind the false wall in the Melody Lounge at the fire's original point. The floor plans submitted in Reilly's report did not indicate this room. The compressor-condenser from the refrigerator unit was removed from the lounge during the investigation and subsequently disappeared. Jack Deady, moreover, believes photos of the northwest corner of the lounge show that fire started behind the wall and burned into the room.

The theory intrigued fire professionals. In 1996, Doug Beller, an NFPA modeling specialist, created a computer model of the Cocoanut Grove case that examined the methyl chloride theory. He found that it explained some of the lingering mysteries of the fire. Methyl chloride may act as a depressive—victims talked about becoming sluggish and passing out. The gas emits a sweet odor—something many victims remarked upon. Short-term exposure causes a bluish skin color; many victims were found with a bluish skin tone thought to be oxygen deprivation. Methyl chloride's thermal decomposition products include phosgene, the gas suspected of causing the pulmonary edema in patients. And alcohol may enhance the chemical's toxic effects.

But Beller noted that methyl chloride is heavier than air and thus would not explain flames seen in the palm tree fronds nor the rolling waves of fire that spread along the ceiling of the lounge and the main dining room. According to a 1993 Boston Fire Department statement to the National Fire Protection Agency, the density of methyl chloride is 1.7 times greater than air and "is inconsistent with this gas causing the observed spread of fire along the ceiling in the Melody Lounge." Ultimately, Beller could not come to a conclusion.

Exactly what occurred that night may never be fully known. Many firefighters, including several who fought the blaze, believe the most logical explanation is still the busboy's match. Witness Maurice Levy, who lost his wife in the fire, was furious at the Boston Fire Department's 1970 report; he angrily told a reporter that he had seen how the fire started and that "my testimony was completely ignored." Casey C. Grant, assistant vice president of codes and standards for the NFPA, who has written and lectured on the Cocoanut Grove fire, believes a combination of factors may have been at work, a "classic example of the complexities and amazing dynamics of fire." Because of the passage of time, the exact synergy that created the inferno will, he fears, never be known.

None of the lingering mysteries helped ease Stanley Tomaszewski's private hell. Tomaszewski went on to school, military duty, a marriage, and career, never shaking the stigma of being "the busboy with the match" and a murderer in the eyes of some. A few years before his death, Tomaszewski told a reporter, "I wish people would let a dead horse die. I've suffered enough—spit on, called every name in the book and threatened. Phone calls in the middle of the night. It hasn't been easy." Yet "I don't have a sense of guilt, because it wasn't my fault. If I felt guilty I wouldn't be talking to you, my name would not be on the doorbell and in the telephone book. I never backed away." Tomaszewski died on October 20, 1994, at the age of sixty-eight, still haunted by the demons that he may—or may not—have unleashed.

Tomaszewski bore the lifelong torments that Welansky managed to cheat through death. Whether the match or methyl chloride caused the fire, no matter whether strange gasses were released by the furnishings or by a mysterious chemical, the major causes of death in the Grove were the locked doors, inadequate exits, and crowded conditions. Whatever the initial spark, greed and thoughtlessness were the real killers.

CHAPTER EIGHT

The Long Road to Recovery

Included in the list of the dead on the front page of the *Boston Globe* on November 29, 1942, were the names of Mr. and Mrs. Martin Sheridan. But Marty was very much alive. In fact, the Nazis had captured him! Even as he drifted in and out of consciousness, agents of the Third Reich were taking blood for experimentation. That's why he couldn't see anything—his face and hands were wrapped in bandages. But he could sense people bustling around him, using words like *edema* and *intravenous.* "You can't fool me with those medical terms," he whispered weakly as he drifted back to sleep. Hours later, when he began to regain consciousness, he recognized the voice of a friend, a doctor. He began to remember being at the Cocoanut Grove and haltingly mouthed questions like "Where is my wife?" "Everything is going to be all right," the doctor said nervously and excused himself. Only after a few days did Sheridan's father gently tell him that his wife, Connie, had not made it out alive; Buck Jones and most of the party of movie executives and their wives were also dead. Sheridan was severely burned on the face and hands, but he would live.

Against all expectations, twenty-year-old Clifford Johnson survived the night at Boston City Hospital. His body had been sprayed with the triple dye and nurses managed to find a vein to give him plasma. When he was still alive after four days, doctors decided they were morally obligated to do everything in their power to help someone with such an incredible will to live. While 45 percent of his skin had been lost to third-degree burns and another 15 to 20 percent had second-degree burns, Johnson's lungs did not have major damage and his still-handsome face was unscathed. Six special nurses were assigned to him and he was placed in a special unit for round-the-clock care. Fortunately, Johnson remained mostly unconscious; when he awoke, it was to a nightmare of pain and delirium. Somehow, he clung to life, battling off a kidney infection, edema, and high fever—he lost more than sixty pounds as protein leached through his system. He hung on and miraculously began to feel better. Doctors now believed he could live, if only his skin could be restored.

So his team began the painstaking task of skin grafts; they took pinpricks of skin from the few unburned spots on Johnson's body and planted them on the burned areas. About six thousand such pinprick grafts were made while Johnson was positioned facedown for six months. Once his upper torso was done, the guardsman, anxious to be in a new position, was turned over. But Johnson had been turned too quickly, within a day, every one of the back skin grafts shifted and sloughed off; all would have to be redone. The blow was devastating to doctors; Johnson, who had valiantly endured the terrible pain and discomforting position, now became suicidal. Yet he endured another twenty-five to thirty-five thousand pinprick skin drafts, and even kicked a terrible addiction to the painkiller codeine in the process. Every day the grafts, hardened to tough leather, had to be rubbed with coconut butter to improve elasticity. His unused legs and arms limbered up with physical therapy. To the amazement of his doctors, he improved.

On July 28, 1943, Johnson stood for the first time in nine months. His natural ability at flirtation had returned with his strength, and the guardsman was eating up attention from nurses and female visitors. When he was finally discharged from the hospital in November of 1945, his rapturous doctors told reporters, "We learned more from him about the treatment of burns than has ever been learned from any other single patient." He returned home to Missouri, but came back to Boston City Hospital one more time—to fight a recurring bone infection. There he met and wooed a student nurse named Marion Donovan. They were married on September 10, 1946, and moved to Missouri.

Clifford Johnson's miraculous story ends on a terrible note. In December of 1956, the thirty-four-year-old Johnson was working as a park warden when his Jeep crashed into a ditch and rolled over, pinning him and spraying him with gasoline. Gas also hit the hot engine and ignited, engulfing the vehicle. Johnson burned to death.

A happier story is that of "Patient 13," as she was described in medical articles, the most severely burned patient to survive at MGH. Shirley Freedman and her date, Lester Gould, had been leaving the Melody Lounge when the fire broke out; she was knocked down several times as she scrambled for the revolving door. She could feel the flames hissing on her legs before she lost consciousness. Gould died in the fire. Freedman survived, but she had burns over 56 percent of her body, including her face, and the fingers of her right hand were destroyed. Her burns were so extensive that she needed general anesthesia when her dressings were changed, and she was nauseated for twenty-four hours afterward. In despair over her ravaged face and body, she refused to eat, her will to live fading. Surgeon Bradford Cannon managed to infuse the young woman with hope, convincing her she had many reasons to carry on. With his encouragement, she began to accept nourishment. She endured nine surgeries and numerous skin grafts that kept her hospitalized for five months.

After her discharge the former Patient 13 married Elliott Harris, a Rhode Island salesman, who, she said, "never saw the scars." She never forgot Dr. Cannon's care and compassion. Years later, her son Jeffrey Bradford Harris, a co-pilot, began flying with Captain Laurie Cannon and discovered, to his amazement, that his pilot was the son of Dr. Cannon. Mrs. Freedman Harris wrote to the aging doctor to thank him for convincing her to carry on. She added, "I am 72 years old today and still fascinated with the mystery of life."

The true comeback kid was singer Dotty Myles. Young Dorothy had extensive burns on her face and hands, severe shock, and a cardiac condition that complicated her recovery. A Red Cross report predicted that she "may never sing again and if she ever plays the piano in the future, it will not be for a long, long time." As she recovered, scars formed over her face and hands, turning her features into a ghastly surface of pockmarks and cracks. Webs of skin extended to her neck, and her hands were stiff and useless. As the weeks went by, she endured skin graft after skin graft, lying in bed and using the rings on the bed curtain like beads of a rosary. She drew strength from meeting Charles Kenney, the fireman who had rescued her and had suffered such severe lung injuries that he had to retire from the fire department. On her eighteenth birthday, March 2, she even tried to sing. Though her voice was weak, she had not lost it. After six months in Boston City Hospital, she was discharged.

Even if she had to give up performing in public, she could still sing. Wearing a veil and gloves, she made the rounds of Boston radio stations, where she was hired to do live broadcasts, including the popular WBZ show "Styles by Myles." She began to receive letters from servicemen who had heard her story and praised her determination. Famed newspaper columnist Damon Runyon, in a 1944 column, cited Dorothy Metzger's courage, writing, "The only fighters are not those in Normandy and the jungles of the Pacific. We've got some great warriors on the home front." Then Myles was introduced to Dr. Varaztad H. Kazanjian, an Armenian immigrant and dentist turned plastic surgeon. While setting jaw fractures, Kazanjian had developed new ways of treating jaw injuries. During World War I he was able to use his skill in prosthetic dentistry to reconstruct the faces of soldiers disfigured during combat. In 1941 he became the first professor of plastic surgery at the Harvard Medical School. And now he was willing to help a victim of the Cocoanut Grove fire. After a long examination, Dr. Kazanjian uttered the words that sent a surge of hope through Dorothy: "There's nothing to worry about so far as your face is concerned. You can be a beautiful girl again."

Myles underwent seventeen operations to rebuild her face. By now all of Boston was rooting for the woman called "Dauntless Dotty." Wearing gloves and with minimal scarring at her throat, she was able to return to a singing career, even appearing in early TV shows in Boston. In the late 1940s and early 1950s, using the name Dorothy McManus (her mother's maiden name), Dotty discovered another career: singing Irish ballads with Irish bands, including a young Joe Derrane and Connie Foley, in Boston's dance halls. She even recorded several records for the Copley record label, with an accent so real that many assumed she was born and raised in Ireland. By the late 1950s, she resumed

Dotty Myles, shown here before she was badly burned in the fire, resumed her career after a number of surgeries. (Courtesy of Charles Kenney)

singing in clubs in New York City. Walter Winchell, in his syndicated column, highlighted Myles's appearance as the "show-stopper" at the Velvet Room, adding, "Champions, as the saying goes, always get up for one more round."

After the fire, Mickey Alpert returned to New York City, where he married his longtime girlfriend (who had herself, ironically, been badly burned in another fire) in the home of mutual friend Milton Berle. He launched a career in variety television as a casting director and worked for Berle's "Texaco Star Theatre," Jackie Gleason, and Ed Sullivan. But he could never escape his memories of the fire. He never talked about that terrible night, but his daughter, Jane, said that as she was growing up, the fire lurked in the shadows of their family life. Mickey Alpert died in 1965, at the age of sixty-one. His brother, George Alpert, went on to become president of the New York–New Haven Railroad and a distinguished corporate attorney. (George's son Richard Alpert became the counterculture guru Baba Ram Dass.)

Five days after the Cocoanut Grove fire, John Quinn was a guard of honor at Dick Vient's funeral; an hour later he was a pallbearer at Marion Luby's funeral. With his burns still healing, he shipped out a week later, and never saw his beloved Gerry again. Quinn came home from the war, a survivor of fire, war, and heartbreak. He went on to civilian life, a marriage, and children. Like many survivors, he could not speak of that night in the Grove for years. Then, in 1998, his recollection of the fire was printed in *Yankee* magazine. Days later he got a call from the man who had married Gerry. Gerry had since died, but the man wanted to thank Quinn profusely for his actions that night.

Jack Lesberg suffered damage to his lungs and esophagus. For weeks after the fire he coughed up black soot. He was hospitalized for about a month and for years afterward suffered anxiety attacks in crowded places. He returned to the burned-out club to see if by some miracle his bass had survived; it had not. He sought a fresh start in New York City and embarked on a long and successful career as a jazz musician, playing with some of the greatest names in the music business, from Louis Armstrong to Leonard Bernstein. Lesberg continued to perform well into his eighties. As for the fire's lingering impact, he said simply, "I got to think of myself as a lucky guy."

Other survivors resumed their careers: Romeo Ferrara continued to play jazz; chorus girl "Pepper" Russell (Henrietta Siegel) opened a dancing school outside Boston. She didn't marry her resuscitated beau Al Willet, who had a long musical career, but the pair stayed friends for life. Jackie Maver worked as a waitress for years in the Boston area. Welansky's nephew Daniel Weiss, who finished medical school and had a distinguished career as a prominent psychiatrist, continued to defend his uncle for the rest of his life.

Buck Jones's body was shipped to California. At his funeral cowboy friends and actors sang his favorite songs, and Monogram vice president Ren Carr described how Jones courageously ran back into the fire twice to rescue patrons—a bit of Hollywood hype that eased the sorrow of his grief-stricken widow and daughter. Within a week of the fire, Boston movie theaters, "answering the requests of thousands," began showing Buck Jones's last picture: *Dawn on the Great Divide*.

Martin Sheridan was hospitalized for two months, fighting off a series of life-threatening infections and complications. He received so

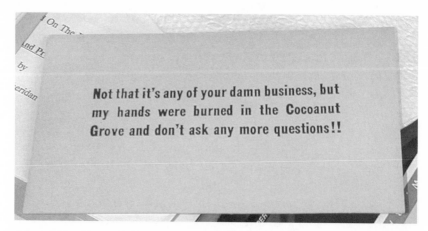

Not that it's any of your damn business, but my hands were burned in the Cocoanut Grove and don't ask any more questions!!

Martin Sheridan, who had to wear gloves to keep infection from his hands as they were healing, printed cards to hand to the curious. (Photo by the author)

Martin Sheridan in 2002. (Photo by the author)

many shots he began to feel like a colander. Skin was shaved from his thighs to create grafts for his hands. Nurses had to spend two hours every day removing scabs from his face, neck, and ears. He was finally discharged in January 1943 but ordered to wear white gloves to keep infection from his still-healing hands. He printed up cards he passed out liberally when asked about the gloves: "Not that it's any of your damn business, but my hands were burned in the Cocoanut Grove and don't ask any more questions!!" After a period of depression, he decided that after surviving the Cocoanut Grove, he would have no fears about being at the war front.

The *Boston Globe* sent him to cover action in the Pacific. Aboard the USS *Fremont* in October of 1944, nine thousand miles from Boston, a young sailor approached him, asking, "Are you Martin Sheridan?"

"Who wants to know?" Sheridan replied.

"I'm the guy who pulled you out of the Cocoanut Grove fire," said Howard Sotherden, now an electrician's mate, first class. He explained that when he pulled out an unconscious man he heard someone exclaim, "Why, it's Marty Sheridan." By coincidence the two wound up on the same ship, and became lifelong friends.

After the war, newspaperman Martin Sheridan pursued a writing and public-relations career in Chicago; he eventually retired to Connecticut. He married, had children, and his children had children. He found great irony in his sudden popularity after the February 2002 Station nightclub fire in Rhode Island, when a new breed of reporters called him for comment. Until his death at age eighty-nine, Sheridan would not let a major anniversary of the fire pass without writing an article or hounding Boston media about acknowledging the anniversary of the Cocoanut Grove fire. He never forgot and he never wanted Boston to forget.

CHAPTER NINE

The Legacy of the Cocoanut Grove

A brass plaque, corroded by Boston's hard winters, is lodged in the sidewalk near the corner of Piedmont and Shawmut streets in the quaint Bay Village neighborhood. The declaration etched into the metal seems disconcertingly upbeat: "Phoenix out of the Ashes," the plaque declares, under a diagram of the doomed nightclub, complete with little palm trees. "As a result of this terrible tragedy major changes were made in the fire codes and improvements in the treatment of burn victims, not only in Boston but across the nation," the plaque declares. Nearby, a garage encompasses the area of the Broadway Lounge; the main dinning room is now a parking lot. The block shows almost no evidence of the gaiety and horror of that terrible Saturday night. Sometimes, however, flowers will appear near the plaque or be tied to the nearby fence—mute testimony of those paying tribute to the dead.

More tangible legacies of the Cocoanut Grove can be seen in public buildings. Four days after the fire, St. Louis, Miami, Cleveland, Philadelphia, Detroit, Des Moines, Chicago, Kansas City, Albany, and Helena, Montana, all changed their fire regulations, according to a United Press report. Today, most states or municipalities require that every revolving door be flanked by regular hinged doors or have such a door nearby. Exits must be clearly marked and must provide a clear

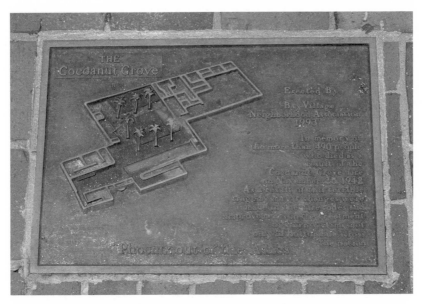

"Phoenix out of the Ashes": the memorial to the Cocoanut Grove, on Piedmont Street, Boston. (Photo by the author)

path to the outside, and exit doors must remain unlocked from the inside and must swing in the direction of exit travel. Emergency lights must have an independent power source. No place of public assembly should be filled beyond its authorized capacity, and such places must have at least two and possibly more exits. No combustible material should be used for decorations.

Yet one of the lingering misconceptions about the fire is that it sparked the creation of many fire-safety codes. But even prior to 1942, the National Fire Protection Association had developed model life-safety codes that covered exits, crowd capacity, and door type. The NFPA already considered revolving doors a "menace." Indeed, "there were few 'new' lessons to be learned from the Cocoanut Grove fire," according to the ninth edition of the *Life Safety Code Handbook*. The fire did inspire more municipalities, Boston foremost among them, to insist on stricter enforcement of codes already on the books. As NFPA official Robert Moulton said, Boston's building codes were at the time of the fire in a "chaotic condition."

Prior to the fire, nightclubs and restaurants were not recognized as places of public assembly—which are subject to stricter codes. The fire changed that definition. In 1943, Massachusetts created the Massachusetts Board of Fire Prevention Regulations, which required municipal fire officials to enforce tougher state codes. The Boston Fire Department also established a position of department chemist, with the responsibility to evaluate draperies and decorations used in nightclubs. Tellingly, the Boston Licensing Board ruled that no place of entertainment in the city could ever again use the name Cocoanut Grove. Thus, the major legacy of the Cocoanut Grove fire on national fire and safety codes was psychological—the fire made local lawmakers more willing to adopt national recommendations.

The medical legacy of the Cocoanut Grove has been well documented. As they struggled to save lives, physicians at Boston City Hospital and Massachusetts General Hospital realized they had a once-in-a-lifetime opportunity to study multiple severe trauma—burns, lung damage, mental anguish—among a cross section of patients, with implications for helping victims of war, explosions, and shipping disasters. Dr. Oliver Cope spearheaded the publication of papers on all aspects of treatment for a 1943 symposium on the medical treatment of Cocoanut Grove patients. Dr. Stanley Levenson and colleagues published several major papers outlining treatments for respiratory trauma. Today, Boston City Hospital has been merged into the Boston University Medical Center, but the burn unit at Massachusetts General Hospital is still known as the country's premiere site for the treatment of burns and other fire-related injuries. Drs. Cope, Moore, Levenson, Lindemann, and Cannon went on to distinguished careers in their respective fields, all profoundly influenced by their Cocoanut Grove experience.

The American rite of exorcism—the court trial—eventually took down only one man: Barnett Welansky. Even amid the calls for accountability, the public and press did not single out those "whose names you won't have to ask for how to spell." Instead, according to the authors of "The Cocoanut Grove Fire: A Study in Scapegoating," published in the *Journal of Abnormal and Social Psychology* in 1943, "People preferred to attack the entire administration set-up rather than certain specific individuals." These authors feared that the fire would spark a wave of anti-Semitism in Boston, as the Welanskys were Jewish, but these fears proved unfounded. Instead, the fire helped establish a major legal prece-dent—that those who maintain unsafe conditions can be prosecuted for manslaughter if deaths occur by their carelessness or inaction. The Cocoanut Grove case has been cited in numerous manslaughter cases, and will probably play a major role in pending legal action surround-ing the deaths of one hundred patrons in the February 2003 Station nightclub fire in Rhode Island.

But mysteries remain. Survivors' tales are confusing and contradic-tory. "I knew some of the people I talked to had fudged their story. They had to. They had to justify their own survival," Paul Benzaquin, who spent several years sorting through numerous interviews for his landmark 1959 book on the fire, told me. "That was a terrible pain for many people—to come out of the fire alive when their dearest, closest people had died." Despite calls to come forward, the man who unscrewed the lightbulb never admitted to his action, nor was he ever identified as being among the dead.

The cynics and writers of letters to the editor were correct: Those who wined and dined for free at the club were never named, much less called to account. For all his vows to "blow the lid" off the Cocoanut Grove, reporter Austen Lake uncovered little besides a sordid, colorful history, which he described in an extravagant style. He fingered no cur-rent politician or official, and he never identified the people who made threats against him, while claiming to "know who they were." As Robert Moulton noted sarcastically in his analysis, "City officials, own-ers of the property, operators of the nightclub and all others who would ordinarily be held responsible have been beautifully exonerated." Often repeated is the story, likely untrue, of Edward "Knocko" McCormack, a bookie and saloon keeper, brother of congressman John W. McCormack, whose daughter died in the fire. When Maurice Tobin came to console Knocko at his daughter's wake, Knocko punched Mayor Tobin in the face.

Welansky, languishing in jail, told a visiting Frank Shapiro, the lawyer working on compensation for survivors, "I was the victim, Frank. I took the blame for the powers and authority at the time." Indeed, Benzaquin believes Welansky was no more corrupt than any other well-connected Bostonian. "He knew the political system. He knew what he could get by on. He used the road that was there."

The site of the Cocoanut Grove nightclub today. The memorial plaque is in the sidewalk. (Photo by the author)

Five years before he died, detective Philip Deady, who had played a major role in investigating the fire, burned all his remaining notes on the case. His son Jack, who has also become a historian of the fire, speculates that he kept the material as "insurance" for years and wonders why his father felt the need to destroy what he had saved for so long. Others, thinking that such an experience could never be forgotten, tossed away the minutiae of the event. Fire department records and police records have been routinely purged. With the consolidation of newspapers in Boston—of the many local Boston daily papers in the 1940s, only the *Globe* and the *Herald* remain—valuable clip files and photographs have been lost or stolen, leaving dark images on microfilm as the only record. Firefighter Charles Kenney never discussed the fire, even with his children, and John Quinn began to tell his story only after fifty years. For Boston-area reporters, covering the Grove was the story of a lifetime, yet none of them wrote a book on the event; they told Benzaquin they figured no one would read a story so horrible. Most victims simply tried their best to forget. As late as 1960, a still-beautiful Dorothy Myles was telling reporters that the fire had not stopped her from pursuing her dream of becoming a singer, yet she never completely overcame the physical and mental trauma of the experience.

As the years went on, repeated myths became established facts. The number of people who "were" going to the club that night until something turned them away has expanded to the point of statistical impossibility. Was an infant in the nightclub at the time of the fire? A witness at the Reilly commission spoke of hearing a woman shriek, "My baby!" and seeing a three-year-old child put in her arms. Apparently, a little boy belonged to a family living on the third floor of the building above the new lounge; he and his family had fled to safety. Was Captain Robert Morgan's famous B-29 bomber *Dauntless Dotty* the first superfortress to bomb Tokyo during World War II, named after Dotty Myles? Myles herself thought so and Morgan, a well-known rake, implied it in a letter he wrote to Dorothy, saying, "I am proud that my plane can carry the same name as yours," according to a United Press story in February of 1945. Yet Morgan, who died in May of 2004, wrote in his biography that the plane was named after his first wife, Dorothy. Mickey Alpert was photographed coming out of the fire wearing a woman's white coat and a look of such horror that his daughter shivered when she looked at the photo decades later. Not even she knows how—or why—Alpert was wearing the coat.

Scott Dunlap, Buck Jones's agent, told a legendary tale. Unconscious from the fumes and smoke, Dunlap awoke to find himself stacked among bodies and someone attempting to get into his pocket. "I'm alive," he managed to cry. "I'll give you three hundred dollars to get me to the hospital." Dunlap heard someone say, "Where's the three hundred?" "In my wallet." Dunlap passed out again; he awoke in a hospital bed. His wallet, which had contained eight hundred dollars, now held five hundred. Dunlap's unusual tale notwithstanding, police reported that looting was a major problem in the aftermath of the fire, and many valuable items disappeared, taken from victims who could ill afford to lose anything.

Difficult as it was to imagine for those directly affected, memories of the fire inevitably faded. On the fiftieth anniversary, the city acknowledged the tragedy with placement of the brass plaque, made by Tony Marra, now a metalworker, who repeated his story of escaping with maple walnut ice cream in his hair. Also attending was the aged but still graceful Jackie Maver, the dancer who led others to safety.

Others will never escape the fire's long reach. In August of 2004, this author sat in the Boston law offices of Friedman and Atherton with ninety-five-year-old attorney Frank H. Shapiro, who was still practicing. As we talked about the fire, Shapiro would occasionally shiver, groan, and put his hands over his face as tears came to his eyes. Images of pulling bodies from the fire still wake him from sleep, still haunt his dreams. "When I get up at night, I think of it. I shudder and try to brush it aside, just like you'd like to close the darkness out," he told me. Despite requests from reporters over the years, Shapiro refuses to discuss all he knows about the "people behind the people behind the people involved" in the case; keeping his mouth shut, he believes, has kept him alive. And now, "what good would it do?" His continued silence reveals how, more than sixty years later, the Cocoanut Grove fire keeps a terrible hold on the imagination of Boston.

ACKNOWLEDGMENTS

This book would not have been possible without the help of many fire professionals, Cocoanut Grove historians, and survivors. My deepest thanks go to Charles Kenney, Jack Deady, Casey Grant, Leo Stapleton, John Quinn, Jack Lesberg, Martin Sheridan, Jane Alpert Bouvier, Paul Christian, Barbara Ravage, Bill Noonan, and John Vahey for their recollections and expertise. Special thanks go to Paul Benzaquin for graciously sharing his memories of writing his extraordinary book on the fire, and also to Boston police archivist Donna Wells and lawyer Frank Shapiro. Thanks also to Sue Marsh and the librarians of the National Fire Protection Association, John Cronin and the staff of the *Boston Herald*, and librarians at the *Boston Globe*, the Medford Public Library, and the Boston Public Library. Very heartfelt kudos go to Donna Halpern for her excellent research assistance. I am grateful for encouragement and guidance from series editor Robert Allison and from Penny Stratton, Katie Bull, and Webster Bull of Commonwealth Editions.

SOURCES

Chapter One: Boston's Number One Glitter Spot

BACKGROUND INFORMATION about the Cocoanut Grove is from Paul Benzaquin, *Fire in Boston's Cocoanut Grove: Holocaust!* (Boston: Branden Press, 1967); Edward Keyes, *Cocoanut Grove* (New York: Atheneum, 1984); Austen Lake, *Galley Slave* (Boston: Burdette and Company, 1965), and articles by Lake in the *Boston Record American*, December 1942; Curt Norris, "N.E. Mysteries," (Quincy, Mass.) *Patriot Ledger*, October 9, 1993; and newspaper articles in the *Boston Daily Globe, Boston Herald, Boston Post, Boston Daily Record, Boston Evening American*, and *Boston Traveler*, November 1942 through January 1943.

Chapter Two: The Day of the Fire

BACKGROUND IN THIS CHAPTER is from my 2003–2004 interviews with Martin Sheridan, Jack Lesberg, John Quinn, Frank Shapiro, and Paul Benzaquin. Also Dorothy Myles, "I Almost Burned to Death," *True Experiences*, October 1948; "Inferno at the Cocoanut Grove," *Yankee*, November 1998; Judy Bass, "No Way Out," *Boston Magazine*, October 1992.

Chapter Three: Into the Inferno

DETAILS ABOUT THE FIRE itself are from "Inferno at the Cocoanut Grove," *Yankee*, November 1998; Casey Cavanaugh Grant, "Last Dance at the Cocoanut Grove," *NFPA Journal*, May/June 1991; John Vahey's analysis of the Cocoanut Grove fire, "Design for Disaster," published in 1982 by the Boston Sparks Association; Robert Moulton's 1943 NFPA report; "Looking Back at the Cocoanut Grove," *Fire Journal*, November 1982; William Arthur Reilly, fire commissioner, city of Boston, "Report Concerning the Cocoanut Grove Fire," November 19, 1943; witness statements from the Boston Police Department archive; and Boston newspaper accounts from November 29 to December 11, 1942.

Chapter Four: Fighting the Blaze

INFORMATION IN THIS CHAPTER is taken from my interviews with Charles Kenney and Jack Deady, and also from Casey Cavanaugh Grant, "Last Dance at the Cocoanut Grove," *NFPA Journal*, May/June 1991; Crowley's letter to Charles Kenney, August 18, 1991, provided courtesy of Kenney and the Crowley family; William Longgood, "After 18 years, singer recalls cry of fire at Cocoanut Grove," *New York World Telegraph and Sun*, December 27, 1960.

Chapter Five: Medical Breakthroughs

MEDICAL INFORMATION ABOUT THE FIRE is from *Symposium on the Management of the Cocoanut Grove Burns at the Massachusetts General Hospital*, 1943, edited by Dr. Oliver Cope and containing fifteen articles from different disciplines on all aspects of the fire, originally published in *Annals of Surgery* 117 (1943); Maxwell Finland, Charles S. Davidson, and Stanley M. Levenson, "Clinical and Therapeutic Aspects of the Conflagration Injuries to the Respiratory Tract Sustained by Victims of the Cocoanut Grove Disaster," *Medicine* 25 (1946): 215–83; Finland, Davidson, and Levenson, "Effects of Plasma and Fluid on Pulmonary Complications in Burned Patients: Studies of the Effects in Victims of the Cocoanut Grove," *Archives of Internal Medicine* 77, no. 5, May 1946; Barbara Ravage, *Burn Unit: Saving Lives after the Flames* (Cambridge, Mass.: Da Capo Press, 2004); Francis Moore, *A Miracle and a Privilege* (Washington, D.C.: National Academy Press, 1995); Atul Gawande, "Desperate Measures," *New Yorker*, May 5, 2003; Oliver Cope, "The End of the Tannic Acid Era," and Thomas H. Coleman, "A Hush on the Brick Corridor," both in *Harvard Medical Alumni Bulletin*, Winter 1991/1992; John C. Sheehan and Robert N. Ross, "The Fire that Made Penicillin Famous," *Yankee*, November 1982; Gloria Negri, "A wing and a prayer reunion," *Boston Globe*, November 14, 1994.

Chapter Six: The Aftermath, Investigation, and Trial

INFORMATION IN THIS CHAPTER is from my interview with Frank Shapiro, and from articles in the *Boston Herald, Globe, Post, Traveler, Record American, Advertiser*, and the *Christian Science Monitor*. Also "Venerable Lawyer Still Holds Secret to Famed '42 Fire," *Massachusetts Lawyers Weekly*, June 2, 1997.

Chapter Seven: What Caused the Fire?

SOURCES INCLUDE INTERVIEWS with Charles Kenney, Jack Deady, Paul Christian, and Casey Grant; Doug Beller and Jennifer Sapochetti, "Searching for Answers to the Cocoanut Grove Fire of 1942," *NFPA Journal*, May/June 2000; Charles Kenney, "The Initial Accelerant" (unpublished monograph); research notes from Jack Deady; Charles Kenney, "Did a Mystery Gas Fuel the Cocoanut Grove Fire?" *Firehouse*, May 1999; *Boston Herald* and *Globe* articles.

Chapter Eight: The Long Road to Recovery

SOURCES INCLUDE MY INTERVIEW with and unpublished manuscripts from Martin Sheridan; interview with Jack Lesberg; details of Clifford Johnson's ordeal from Paul Benzaquin's account in *Life*, August 31, 1959, and Benzaquin, *Fire in Boston's Cocoanut Grove*.

Chapter Nine: The Legacy of the Cocoanut Grove

SOURCES INCLUDE INTERVIEWS with Paul Benzaquin, Frank Shapiro, and Casey Grant. Information on code changes is from NFPA publications and files. The background on the fiftieth anniversary is from news articles, including "Tragedy is commemorated: Ceremony at Cocoanut Grove site sees bittersweet reunion," *Boston Globe*, November 29, 1992; "Cocoanut Grove 50-year ceremony set," *Boston Herald*, November 27, 1992.

INDEX

Note: Bold numbers indicate pages with photographs or drawings.